Library of
Davidson College

U.S. ECONOMIC POLICIES AFFECTING INDUSTRIAL TRADE

A Quantitative Assessment

BY PETER MORICI
AND LAURA L. MEGNA
Assisted by SARA N. KRULWICH

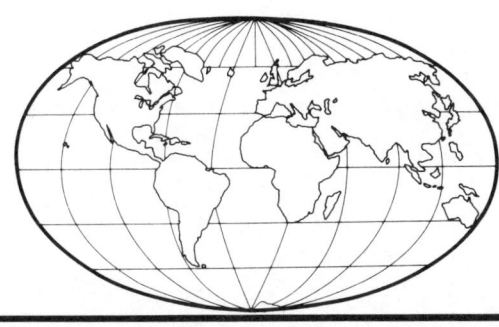

NPA Committee on
Changing International Realities

330.973
M 854u

U.S. Economic Policies Affecting Industrial Trade:
A Quantitative Assessment

CIR Report #13
NPA Report #200

Price $12.00

ISBN 0-89068-068-X
Library of Congress
Catalog Card Number 83-60013

Copyright 1983   83-4137
by the National Planning Association
A voluntary association incorporated under the laws
of the District of Columbia
1606 New Hampshire Avenue, N.W.
Washington, D.C. 20009

Contents

U.S. Economic Policies Affecting Industrial Trade: A Quantitative Assessment
by Peter Morici and Laura L. Megna
assisted by Sara N. Krulwich

NPA's Committee on Changing International Realities and Their Implications for U.S. Policy	*inside front cover*
A Statement by the Committee	vii
Members of the Committee Signing the Statement	ix
Introduction	1

Chapter 1 Trade-Distorting Practices and U.S. Trade Policy — 4
What Is a Trade-Distorting Practice? — 4
Factors Influencing Postwar Trade Policy — 5
The Resulting Tariff Structure — 8
Nontariff Barriers — 10

Chapter 2 TDPs Affecting Producer and Consumer Prices — 14
Quantitative Restrictions — 14
  Nonrubber Footwear — 15
  Color Televisions — 18
  Carbon Steel and Specialty Steel — 20
  Textiles and Apparel — 22
  Automobiles — 24
  Nondramatic Literary Publications — 27
Safeguard (Escape Clause) Actions — 28
Customs Valuation — 30
  U.S. Valuation System Prior to 1980 — 32
  Post-Tokyo Round Customs Valuation Procedures — 32
  Impact of the Customs Valuation Code on
    U.S. Valuation Procedures — 33
  Tariff Nomenclatures — 35
  Costs Imposed by U.S. Customs Documentation
    Requirements — 36
Excise Taxes — 37
Government Procurement — 37
  Direct Federal Procurement — 39
  State and Local Government Procurement — 40
  Assessing the Effects of Buy-National Policies — 41
  The Effects of the GATT Government
    Procurement Code — 41
Product Standards — 42
  Product Standards as NTBs — 42
  U.S. Product Standards — 43
  The Tokyo Round's "Standards Code" — 46
Overview — 46
  Outlook for 1985 — 46

	Sectoral Data	47
	Practices of other AICs	49
Chapter 3	**Domestic Production Subsidies**	**54**
	General Programs	55
	Adjustment Assistance to Firms and Regional Development Programs	55
	Tax Incentives for R&D	60
	Crude Oil and Natural Gas Price Regulations	62
	Industrial Revenue Bonds	64
	Industry-Specific Programs	64
	Shipbuilding	65
	Footwear	66
	Other Programs	68
	Overview	70
	Outlook for 1985	71
	Comparison with Other AICs	71
Chapter 4	**Export Promotion**	**76**
	Export Credits	76
	Export Credit Competition	77
	U.S. Export Credits	77
	Overseas Private Investment Corporation	80
	Tax Incentives Provided by Domestic International Sales Corporations	83
	Tied Aid	85
	Other Export Promotion Programs	87
	Overview	88
	Potential Implication of Export Disincentives	88
	Outlook for 1985	89
	Sectoral Data	89
	Comparison with Other AIC Export Promotion Programs	89
Chapter 5	**Conclusions**	**97**
	U.S. Nontariff Barriers and the Structure of Protection	98
	Comparison of U.S. Protection to that of Other AICs	101
	Outlook for 1985	103
Appendix A	**Data Sources**	**105**
Appendix B	**What Is a Trade Distortion?**	**109**
Appendix C	**Methodology**	**111**
	TDPs Affecting Producer and Consumer Prices	111
	Domestic Production and Export Subsidies	116
	Quality of Estimates and the Study's Overall Conclusions	121
Appendix D	**Methodology for Estimating the Tariff Equivalents of Discriminatory Government Procurement**	**124**
	National Planning Association	**128**

NPA Officers and Board of Trustees 129

Recent NPA Publications *inside back cover*

Tables

1- 1.	Average *Ad Valorem* U.S. Tariffs by Major SIC Sector	9
1- 2.	Average *Ad Valorem* U.S. Tariffs: Quartiles Ranked by Value-Added per Employee	10
1- 3.	Summary Findings: Estimated Tariff and Subsidy Equivalents of U.S. Industrial Trade-Distorting Practices	11
2- 1.	Major U.S. Quantitative Restrictions of Industrial Imports	15
2- 2.	U.S. Nonrubber Footwear Market	16
2- 3.	U.S. Nonrubber Footwear Imports	17
2- 4.	Consumption and Imports of Complete and Incomplete Color Televisions	19
2- 5.	U.S. Apparel Consumption and Imports	23
2- 6.	Domestic and Import Shares of the U.S. Passenger Automobile Market	25
2- 7.	U.S. Safeguard Actions in Place and Their Estimated Tariff Equivalents	31
2- 8.	Distribution of Customs Entries by Bases of Valuation	33
2- 9.	Protection Provided by ASP Valuation	35
2-10.	Additional Protection Provided by Final List by Major SIC Sector	35
2-11.	Products with 1976 Imports Over $25 Million Whose Duties Were Raised at Least 1 Percent by Final List	36
2-12.	Estimated Additional Tax and Duty Collected	38
2-13.	Summary of Protection Provided U.S. Manufactures by NTBs Affecting Producer and Consumer Prices	47
2-14.	Tariff Equivalents of NTBs that Affect Producer and Consumer Prices by Major SIC Sector	48
3- 1.	Summary: Major Incentives to Domestic Manufacturing	56
3- 2.	Sectoral Summary of Adjustment Assistance to Firms and Regional Development Program Authorizations	58
3- 3.	Domestic Production Subsidies	59
3- 4.	Company R&D Funds	61
3- 5.	Shipbuilding Incentive Programs	66
3- 6.	Allocation of Footwear Industry Revitalization Program Assistance	67
3- 7.	Estimated Annual Savings to Footwear Industry from Technical Assistance	67
3- 8.	Summary of Protection Extended by Domestic Production Subsidies	69
3- 9.	Public Assistance to Enterprises in Seven Major Industrial Countries	71
3-10.	Net Benefits to Private and Public Enterprises in the Major AICs	73
4- 1.	A Comparison of Export Credits Provided by the United States and Other Major Countries	78
4- 2.	EXIM Authorizations	79
4- 3.	EXIM Authorizations by Major SIC Sector	80
4- 4.	Estimated Rates of Subsidy Provided by Selected U.S. Export Promotion Programs by Major SIC Sector	81
4- 5.	Reagan Administration 1983 Budget Estimates and Proposals for EXIM	81
4- 6.	OPIC-Assisted Activities	82
4- 7.	Reagan Administration Budget Estimates and Proposals for OPIC	82
4- 8.	DISC Activities	83
4- 9.	U.S. Budget Authority for Foreign Assistance	85
4-10.	AID-Financed Expenditures on U.S. Commodities	86

4-11.	A Comparison of International Export Marketing Expenditures	88
4-12.	A Comparison of International Market Promotion Strategies	90
4-13.	Summary of Subsidies to U.S. Manufactured Exports	92
4-14.	Summary of Relative Export Incentives to Manufacturing in the United States and Other Major AICs	92
4-15.	Bilateral Aid as a Percent of U.S. and Other Major AIC Merchandise Exports	93
5- 1.	Tariff and Subsidy Equivalents of U.S. Industrial Trade-Distorting Practices	98
5- 2.	Selected U.S. Industrial NTB Tariff Equivalents by Major SIC Sector	100
5- 3.	Average Estimated Protection Provided U.S. Industry: Quartiles Ranked by Value-Added per Employee	101
5- 4.	Post-Kennedy Round Average Industrial Tariff Rates: Seven Major Industrial Countries	102
A- 1.	Selected Manufacturing Data	107
A- 2.	Loan and Loan Guarantee Terms	108
C- 1.	Selected U.S. Industrial NTB Tariff Equivalents Evaluated at R + 2%, by Major SIC Sector	119
D- 1.	U.S. Federal Direct Procurement of Goods and Services	126
D- 2.	Estimates of Imports Excluded by Federal Buy-National Policies	126

Figures

1-1.	Trade-Distorting Practices	6
2-1.	Safeguard Actions Taken by Various Governments	29
C-1.	The Impact of a Tariff	112
C-2.	The Impact of a PCP Nontariff Barrier	113

A Statement by the Committee on Changing International Realities

Since its founding in 1975, the Committee on Changing International Realities has been concerned about the ever more intense competition faced by U.S. firms in international markets. Rising import penetration in established manufacturing sectors, such as textiles and apparel, footwear, automobiles, and steel, as well as the growing challenge to U.S. leadership in high technology activities, make the long-term competitive viability of American industry one of the most critical public policy questions of the 1980s. Indeed, with the United States increasingly dependent on international markets, the competitive viability of U.S. industry is crucial to achieving high levels of employment, to increasing productivity and to raising standards of living. Consequently, the CIR has sought to play a constructive role by sponsoring a series of studies examining the determinants of competitiveness, and this study by Peter Morici and Laura L. Megna, assisted by Sara N. Krulwich, is the sixth in this series.

In recent years, public policymakers, opinion leaders and scholars have become increasingly concerned about the roles of domestic and international economic policies in the United States, Japan, Western Europe, Canada, and emerging developing countries in determining the structure of competitiveness in world markets. In particular, as tariffs have been reduced through successive rounds of GATT-sponsored multilateral trade negotiations, attention has increasingly turned to the role of nontariff trade-distorting practices, including nontariff barriers to imports, export incentives and other programs designed to support or promote domestic employment in selected sectors. Concern has emerged that the influence of these practices has grown to the point that it now may exceed tariffs in importance.

Since the ultimate impacts of government policies on competitiveness are often the result of the interaction of many individual public-sector initiatives, the authors were asked to examine the full range of U.S. domestic and international economic policies affecting trade in manufactured products. In particular, they were asked to conduct an exhaustive review of these policies and, wherever possible, estimate the tariff-equivalents of measures discouraging imports and the implicit subsidies afforded by programs encouraging exports and domestic production; further, wherever possible, they were asked to compare U.S. practices with those of the other major industrial countries.

The study's terms of reference presented the authors with a considerable challenge. Such an exhaustive empirical study of a major industrial country's policies affecting trade was unprecedented. The authors readily admit that many of their estimates of the effects of particular practices in specific industries are approximate. Nevertheless, they believe their results, at the aggregate level for the average levels of protection of U.S. industry, are useful and provide preliminary evidence that support the following conclusions. First, across the full spectrum of manufacturing, the average additional protection provided U.S. import-competing industries by nontariff trade-distorting practices does not appear to have grown to the same importance as tariffs. Second, U.S. programs that encourage exports appear to provide benefits that are no greater, and probably less, than the protection received by import-competing industries. Third, the combined effects of two of three major groups of U.S. practices studied—domestic production subsidies and export incentives—appear to provide significantly fewer benefits than those of most other major advanced industrial countries. Fourth, the overall protection provided by U.S. nontariff trade-distorting practices, like tariffs, appears to be declining.

We believe that, at this critical point in the evolution of the U.S. economy and the international trading system, careful evaluation of the full range of domestic and international economic policies and the interrelationships between them are critical. The data and analysis provided by this study should substantially contribute to an understanding of the important trade-policy issues of the day and are worthy of the attention of private- and public-sector decisionmakers and concerned citizens. Accordingly, regardless of whether we, as individuals, agree or disagree with all of the study's specific interpretations and conclusions, we believe it makes a very important and timely contribution to our understanding of the serious economic policy questions confronting the nation. We are therefore pleased to recommend that it be published by NPA as a report signed by its authors.

Members of the Committee on Changing International Realities Signing the Statement

J.G. CLARKE
Chairman; Director & Senior Vice President, Exxon Corporation

ROBERT R. FREDERICK
Chairman of the Executive Committee; President, RCA Corporation

MARION H. ANTONINI
Group Vice President & President, International Operations, Xerox Corporation

LEE S. APPLETON
Regional Vice President, East, Allis-Chalmers Corporation

HOWARD W. BELL
Director & Financial Vice President, Standard Oil Company of California

GEORGE J. CLARK
Executive Vice President, Citibank, N.A.

J.E. CONNOR
Chairman & Senior Partner, Price Waterhouse

JOHN R. COX
President, INA Corporation

J.W. DAVISON
Senior Vice President, Phillips Petroleum Company

DONALD J. DONAHUE
Vice Chairman & Operations Officer, The Continental Group, Inc.

GEORGE T. FARRELL
President, Mellon Bank N.A.

MURRAY H. FINLEY
President, Amalgamated Clothing & Textile Workers' Union

RAYMOND G. FISHER
Business Consultant, Greenwich, Connecticut

FRANCIS G. FOSTER, JR.
Vice President, Alumax, Inc.

RICHARD W. FOXEN
Vice President, International, Rockwell International Corp.

IRVING S. FRIEDMAN
Senior Advisor, The First Boston Corporation

THEODORE GEIGER
Distinguished Research Professor of Intersocietal Relations, School of Foreign Service, Georgetown University

RALPH W. GOLBY
Vice President, Investor Relations, Schering-Plough Corporation

ROGER W. GRAY
Professor and Economist, Food Research Institute, Stanford University

JAMES R. GREENE
President, American Express International Banking Corporation

ROBERT A. HANSON
President, Deere and Company

ROBERT T. HOLMES
President, International Group, Burroughs Corporation

JOHN H. JACKSON
Professor of Law, The University of Michigan Law School

G. GRIFFITH JOHNSON
Executive Vice President, Motion Picture Association of America, Inc.

LEONARD KAMSKY
Senior Vice President, W.R. Grace and Company

PETER F. KROGH
Dean, Edmund A. Walsh School of Foreign Service, Georgetown University

BARRY J. MASON
Executive Vice President, Republic National Bank of Dallas

JOHN MILLER
Vice Chairman, National Planning Association

WILLIAM R. MILLER
President, Pharmaceutical & Nutritional Group, Bristol-Myers Company

ALFRED F. MIOSSI
Executive Vice President, Continental Illinois National Bank & Trust Company of Chicago

WILLIAM S. OGDEN
Vice Chairman & Chief Financial Officer, The Chase Manhattan Bank, NA.

DAVID R. PARKER
Senior Vice President & Sector Executive, Worldwide Metal Packaging, American Can Company

RALPH A. PFEIFFER, JR.
Chairman of the Board, Far East Corporation/IBM World Trade Americas

MYER RASHISH
Washington, D.C.

THOMAS A. REED
Group Vice President, International Control Systems, Honeywell Inc.

WILLIAM D. ROGERS
Partner, Arnold & Porter

JOHN ROORDA
Vice President, Planning, Shell Oil Company

HERBERT SALZMAN
Westport, Connecticut

NATHANIEL SAMUELS
Chairman, Advisory Director, Lehman Brothers Kuhn Loeb

DANIEL I. SARGENT
General Partner, Salomon Brothers

Committee Signers

MARK SHEPHERD, JR.
Chairman of the Board & Chief Executive Officer, Texas Instruments Incorporated

WILLIAM F. SPENGLER
President & Chief Operating Officer, Domestic Operations, Owens-Illinois

WALTER STERLING SURREY
Senior Partner, Surrey and Morse

ALEXANDER C. TOMLINSON
President, National Planning Association

THOMAS N. URBAN
President & Chief Executive Officer, Pioneer Hi-Bred International

MARK H. WILLES
Executive Vice President & Chief Financial Officer, General Mills, Inc.

ROBERT A. WILSON
Vice President, Public Affairs, Pfizer, Inc.

CHARLES G. WOOTTON
Senior Director, Public Affairs, Gulf Oil Corporation

The opinions expressed and the recommendations presented in the Committee Statement are solely those of the individual members of the Committee on Changing International Realities whose signatures are offered hereto and do not represent the views of the National Planning Association or its staff.

Introduction

Through most of the post-World War II period, the United States has promoted the formation of a more open international trade and payments system and supported the development aspirations of Third World nations. To these ends, it participated in the establishment and efforts of the General Agreement on Tariffs and Trade (GATT), the International Monetary Fund (IMF), the World Bank, and other international institutions. Promoting freer trade and capital flows were key elements of a U.S. policy to encourage economic reconstruction and development among the advanced industrial and developing economies. This policy, in turn, was part of a broader U.S. strategy to promote economic and political security and contain Soviet expansionism.

The advanced industrialized countries (AICs) emerged from World War II with high and complex tariff structures by today's standards. The competitive tariff escalations of the early 1930s were followed by limited bilateral and multilateral negotiations. But these efforts were not enough; excessive levels of protection prevailed throughout the industrial world,[1] and the most-favored-nation (MFN) principle was not generally applied.

Through the establishment of the GATT (1947) and successive rounds of GATT-sponsored multilateral trade negotiations (MTNs), tariffs were lowered substantially between the first round in 1947 and the completion of the Kennedy Round cuts in 1972. During most of this period, the dislocations imposed by trade liberalization were minimized by rapid rates of economic expansion among the AICs. By the early 1970s, tariffs had been lowered to the point that they were no longer perceived by many observers to be the dominant barriers to trade.

During the late 1960s and 1970s, other nontariff trade-distorting practices became the focus of greater attention by policymakers, negotiators and analysts concerned wth trade liberalization. For the first time, the Tokyo Round negotiations (1973-79) devoted as much attention to nontariff measures as to tariffs. In this study, the term nontariff barriers (NTBs) refers to such nontariff trade-distorting practices; it is used to refer to the full range of these policies, including practices that reduce imports, measures that promote exports and programs that do both.

To some extent, concern about NTBs increased because administrative and technical barriers became more obvious as tariffs declined. However, many governments in developed economies increasingly turned to policies designed to ease adjustment or maintain employment in ailing industries and to promote the growth of new activities considered vital to national interests. While it was not always the intention of policymakers to affect trade flows, many of these practices impacted trade by deflecting imports and promoting exports and may be characterized as TDPs (trade-distorting practices) or when they did not involve tariffs, NTBs. The rise of political pressures for new forms of protection is rooted in many factors, among which are—

- Unlike earlier rounds of the GATT negotiations, which eliminated much excessive protection, the Kennedy Round cut deeply into protection that was necessary for the viability of segments of some industries. The additional adjustment problems associated with tariff reductions increased pressures on national governments for other forms of relief from import competition.

- As growth in the industrial economies slowed, the structural adjustments imposed by trade liberalization became more burdensome.

- The burdens arising from structural adjustments were further exacerbated by the growing export competitiveness of the newly industrializing countries (NICs) in selected manufacturing industries and by the structural adjustments imposed by rising energy prices.

While empirical evidence is scarce, many observers believe NTBs have become very important obstacles to trade.[2] It is this need for hard data that precipitated this study.

The study's primary focus is U.S. tariff and nontariff trade-distorting practices. In particular, it briefly reviews the evolution of the U.S. tariff structure from pre-Kennedy Round to post-Tokyo Round levels and examines in detail U.S. NTBs that displace imports and encourage exports.[3] The objective is to provide preliminary estimates of the tariff equivalents of as many U.S. NTBs as possible across the full range of manufacturing industries.

Estimating the tariff equivalents of NTBs is a difficult and inexact exercise, especially when the objective is to obtain measurements across all of a country's practices and manufacturing industries. Many judgments were necessary, and the authors emphasize that many of the results reported here are *order of magnitude estimates* of the restrictive effects of many U.S. NTBs.[4] Nevertheless, since no previous study has attempted such a complete, across-the-board measurement of the effects of NTBs, the authors believe the results presented here, while approximate, are a useful first step in answering several basic questions about the growth and importance of NTBs to the U.S. economy.

Four key questions are addressed. First, to what extent has the importance of U.S. nontariff barriers that reduce imports grown to exceed that of tariffs? Since many U.S. NTBs reducing imports were imposed on a temporary basis and several others were eliminated by the Tokyo Round, the objective here is to measure the additional protection various NTBs afford U.S. manufacturing over and above the standing protection already provided by tariffs. On that basis, the results presented here indicate that, on average across all manufacturing industries, the protection from NTBs that limit or discourage imports has not grown to the same importance as the protection provided by tariffs. As shown in Appendix C, despite the fact that many of the results reported are order of magnitude estimates, the very large differences between the protection due to tariffs and the estimated values of the additional protection provided by NTBs limiting imports indicate that this result is fairly significant.

Second, how does assistance to U.S. exporting industries compare to the protection received by U.S. import-competing industries? The results presented here indicate that the programs and incentives encouraging U.S. exports appear to yield benefits that are no greater, and probably less, than the protection provided import-competing industries by tariff and nontariff barriers to imports.

Third, how do U.S. import protection and export promotion activities compare to the practices of other AICs? Four types of practices are studied here—tariffs, nontariff barriers that affect producer and consumer prices, domestic production subsidies, and export subsidies. For tariffs, domestic production subsidies and export subsidies, comparisons at the aggregate level (e.g., averages across all industries) indicate that, on average, the United States provides its manufacturing sector with significantly less import protection and export incentives than do other AICs. Further, it appears unlikely that the difference between U.S. protection and that of other AICs' NTBs affecting producer and consumer prices would offset this imbalance. Of course, a definitive answer to this question will require similar detailed studies of trade practices in other AICs.

Fourth, what impact have the Tokyo Round and other U.S. trade policy initiatives had on the outlook for the protection received by U.S. manufacturing? The results presented here indicate that over the next several years, the combined protection from U.S. tariff and nontariff barriers appears to be declining because of the implementation of the agreements reached in the Tokyo Round and recent federal budget reductions. By 1985, the protection afforded most manufacturing industries should be significantly reduced from pre-Tokyo Round levels if the United States continues to pursue its present policies.

This study is divided into five chapters. Chapter 1 first defines TDPs and NTBs and presents a brief review of types of NTBs. It then examines the evolution of U.S. trade policy since World War II and briefly analyzes the evolving tariff structure. Chapter 2 examines those NTBs that affect producer and consumer prices, while Chapters 3 and 4 discuss domestic production subsidies and export incentives, respectively. Chapter 5 sets out the conclusions of the study in detail.

Notes

1   These are levels of protection greater than those necessary to maintain the competitiveness of domestic import-competing producers.

2   For example see Bela Balassa, "The New Protectionism and the International Economy," *Journal of World Trade and Law*, September-October 1978; Richard Blackhurst, Nicolas Marian and Jan Tumlir, *Trade Liberalization and Interdependence*, GATT Studies in International Trade (Geneva: GATT, 1977); and Bahram Nowzad, *The Rise of Protectionism*, Pamphlet Series No. 24 (Washington: IMF, 1978).

3   To obtain a balanced and full view of the impacts of a country's policies on trade, it is essential to look at both practices that displace imports and efforts to increase exports.

4   The methodologies employed to estimate tariff equivalents are discussed in Appendix C.

Trade-Distorting Practices and U.S. Trade Policy 1

This discussion begins with a brief exposition of a trade-distorting practice and is intended for the less technical reader; a more rigorous discussion is presented in Appendix B.

WHAT IS A TRADE-DISTORTING PRACTICE?

Prices in international markets have an important influence on how the United States answers two fundamental economic questions:

- what and how much is produced and consumed?

- what and how much is imported and exported?

In the absence of TDPs and domestic market imperfections,[1] a rather precise relationship would exist between international market prices, domestic prices and the patterns of U.S. production, consumption and trade. Of course, such perfect markets have never existed; yet, a description of the price conditions that would prevail provides a useful point of departure for defining exactly what is meant by a TDP.

In the absence of TDPs and domestic market imperfections, domestic consumers could choose between domestic products and imports, where the price of imports would be equal to their f.o.b. export price plus transportation costs and other markups (freight, insurance and so forth). For identical products, the prices consumers paid for domestic and imported products would be equal. Also, the prices consumers paid for exportable commodities would equal their f.o.b. export prices. Therefore, other things remaining the same, prices faced by consumers (P_c) would equal world market prices (P_w).

Similarly, in the absence of domestic market imperfections, the prices received by producers from consumers would equal producers' costs for materials, labor and capital (including a market-determined, risk-adjusted rate of profit).[2] Prices received by producers (P_p) would equal consumers' prices and, in turn, be equal to world prices for exports and imports. In short:

$$P_p \text{ equals } P_c \text{ equals } P_w.$$

Through these price relationships, world prices and market conditions interact with domestic supply and demand conditions to determine what and how much the domestic economy produces, consumes, exports, and imports. A TDP may be defined as a government policy or practice that, *in the absence of other market imperfections or externalities,* upsets the equality of producer, consumer and world prices and thereby changes patterns of exports and imports.³ Tariffs are clearly TDPs and, for the purposes of this study, NTBs are defined to include all other TDPs. It should be noted that not all practices falling within this definition were intended by policymakers when conceived to distort trade (for example, some forms of regional development assistance); nevertheless, they may have this effect.

TDPs may be divided into two groups, and Figure 1-1 presents a list of some of the more significant TDPs applied around the world. First, some TDPs insulate the domestic market by placing a wedge between producer and consumer prices, on the one hand, and world prices, on the other. For example, an import tariff permits domestic firms to produce more, incur higher unit costs and pass these costs on to consumers. The same may be said of various other import barriers, such as quantitative restrictions or arbitrary standards imposed on imports. These practices allow the prices of domestic products to rise above the world price, encouraging additional production, less consumption and less imports.

Second, other TDPs place a wedge between producer prices, on the one hand, and consumer and world prices, on the other. These include domestic production subsidies and export subsidies, which allow domestic producers to incur costs on marginal production in excess of the prices charged consumers, as consumers continue to face world prices. Domestic firms may then produce and sell more at prevailing world prices and displace imports or increase exports.

Under this definition, many broad-based tax and spending programs may be TDPs, making the definition too broad and cumbersome from an empirical perspective and probably unrealistic from a policy standpoint. To narrow the scope of the definition, it may be assumed that broad-based taxes and spending programs are not trade distorting. This assumption is often implicit in theoretical and empirical studies of tariffs and other TDPs. Alternatively, it may be assumed that a social welfare function exists and the government is charged with maximizing it. Under these circumstances, broad-based taxes and spending programs may be viewed as welfare maximizing.

Further, some specific government actions allow domestic producer and/or consumer prices to rise above world prices, but are not TDPs. For example, antidumping and countervailing duties raise the effective price of imports. But these actions are taken in response to TDPs imposed by other countries that artificially lower world prices below the cost of production and, therefore, may be viewed as compensating rather than trade distorting. A similar argument may be made for trade measures taken under Section 301 of the Trade Agreements Act of 1974 in response to unfair trade practices abroad.

Finally, not all barriers to trade are imposed by government. Some are the natural consequence of the distance between countries. These natural protective barriers create natural differences between prices in domestic and foreign markets that are reflected in world prices—the prices of exports and imports faced by domestic producers and consumers. Therefore, they do not drive a wedge between producer and consumer prices and world prices. They are not TDPs or NTBs.

FACTORS INFLUENCING POSTWAR TRADE POLICY

As part of the global tide of protectionism, U.S. tariffs reached their highest levels in this century under the Smoot-Hawley Tariff Act of 1930, which raised the average *ad valorem* rate on dutiable imports to over 50 percent. President Roosevelt began

FIGURE 1-1. TRADE-DISTORTING PRACTICES

(A) Practices affecting producer and consumer prices
  (1) Revenue-generating practices
    Tariffs
    Variables levies
    Excessive fees or charges for service (e.g., parts)
    Import deposits
    Tariff quotas
    Auction quotas
    Arbitrary customs valuation
    Discriminatory applications of excise taxes
  (2) Nonrevenue-generating practices
    Nonauction quotas, orderly marketing agreements and other quantitative restraints
    Discriminatory government procurement
    Excessive import documentation costs and delays
    Arbitrary application of product standards
    State trading
    Split exchange rates
    Performance requirements on foreign investors
    Countertrade and offset agreements

(B) Practices affecting producer prices only
  (1) Direct industry subsidies
    Direct cash grants
    Tax credits, special tax arrangements
    Benefits-in-kind
  (2) Preferential access to credit
    Concessional rates
    Loan guarantees and insurance programs
  (3) State ownership or equity participation at less-than-competitive rates of profit
  (4) Export-specific subsidies
    Subsidized export credit
    Government-financed export promotion
    Tied aid to LDCs
    Loan guarantees for foreign investment
    Tax incentives

reducing tariffs on a reciprocal basis under the authority of the Reciprocal Trade Agreements Act (RTAA) of 1934. The act was renewed 11 times and, until 1962, was the legal basis for U.S. participation in bilateral and multilateral negotiations.

By the time the first GATT negotiations began in 1947, the United States had completed bilateral agreements with 29 countries. So, participation in the GATT MTNs was a natural extension of the reciprocal tariff negotiations begun before the war. However, while the United States was a strong advocate of *freer* trade, it certainly did not pursue a full *free* trade policy in negotiations. Throughout the postwar period, a limited free trade policy was the product of competing forces.

Several important factors encouraged the pursuit of freer trade. First, the experiences of the 1930s made it obvious that across-the-board high levels of protection did not ensure high levels of employment.

Second, a freer trade policy was consistent with the U.S. laissez-faire approach to domestic economic policy. By the late 1940s, the lessons of the depression caused policymakers to accept a role for the federal government in maintaining high levels of employment and growth through monetary and fiscal policy; but active government participation in determining the fortunes of particular industries and labor groups was considered outside the scope of government's legitimate role. No need was perceived for an industrial policy, in which tariffs can be an important element, to guide resource allocation and industrial development.

Third, the United States was committed to the economic reconstruction and development of its industrial allies as part of a foreign policy of promoting the greater economic and political security of the West. The growth of trade through freer access to U.S. markets and lower trade barriers elsewhere was one way of achieving these goals.

Fourth, freer trade was consistent with a U.S. policy of establishing a secure environment for U.S. foreign investment through free capital movements and equitable treatment of U.S. subsidiaries abroad.

Fifth, during the postwar era, academic economists raised policymakers' awareness of the consumer welfare and production efficiency benefits achieved through lower tariffs but significantly deemphasized the adjustment costs imposed on workers and firms in import-competing industries.

Sixth, the rapid rates of economic expansion that characterized the first 25 years of the postwar era made the adjustments imposed by trade liberalization easier to absorb.

While these forces were encouraging freer trade, other constraining factors tempered the pace of tariff reductions. First, U.S. trading partners were not in a position to eliminate tariffs completely and expose their industries to unlimited international competition. Japanese and West European industries were damaged by the war, and the legacy of Canada's long history of protection was an industry too fragmented to compete effectively with U.S. producers without protection. In such an environment, the United States could not successfully pursue an unlimited freer trade policy, although it may be argued that in some cases the United States gave up more than it received in the general reduction of postwar tariffs and the establishment of new trading relationships.[4]

A second constraint involves the dichotomy between the effects of freer trade on consumers and producers. While consumers may benefit from the lower prices and greater product variety that accompany lower tariffs, adjustment burdens and new export opportunities are not evenly distributed among industries, labor groups and regions. Structural adjustments tend to be more difficult for workers in established sectors of the economy where demand usually grows more slowly and production is more intense in less skilled labor (and with lower capital requirements) than elsewhere in the economy. The structural adjustment costs imposed on workers and firms by tariff reductions and the general expansion of trade are important factors in the formulation of U.S. trade policy.

Prior to the 1948 renewal of the RTAA, concern was rising in Congress that the Reciprocal Trade Agreements Program was imposing injury on domestic producers. In response to these sentiments, an *escape clause* requirement and a *peril point provision* were embodied in the 1948 renewal of the RTAA. The peril point provision required the Tariff Commission to establish, *prior to negotiations,* the maximum tariff concessions that could be made without imperiling domestic industry. Tariff concessions in excess of these had to be reported to Congress. Under the escape clause procedure, tariff concessions already in place could be withdrawn on the basis of a Tariff Commission finding of injury.[5]

Until the Trade Expansion Act of 1962, the U.S. approach to negotiations continued to embody the principles of reciprocal concessions *and* the avoidance of injury to domestic firms and workers. The 1962 law provided the legal framework for

U.S. participation in the Kennedy Round and continued the reciprocity principle, but replaced the peril point provision with a promise of adjustment assistance:

> The law no longer required the determination of minimum duties essential to the protection of the industries concerned—the basic characteristic of the old peril-point provision. Although an escape clause was retained, the new law recognized that tariff concessions would cause hardship for certain industries, firms, and workers. With few exceptions, the remedy provided was not to be an upward adjustment of rates, but rather assistance for those concerned with meeting the new competition. In short, it was assumed that in the administration of the act, some industries, firms, and workers could expect to be injured by tariff concessions. This was a reversal of the philosophy of tariff negotiations that had prevailed since 1948.[6]

Thus, the United States became committed to pursuing tariff reductions potentially injurious to domestic industries by promising adjustment assistance to affected firms and workers. Unfortunately, the assistance proved extremely inadequate. It provided *very* limited relief because of strict eligibility requirements—only 18 firms and 52,000 workers received assistance between 1962 and 1974.[7] The lack of an effective adjustment assistance program, coupled with the growth of imports caused by the Kennedy Round tariff reductions and the growing export competitiveness of Japan and the NICs, caused the United States to turn to the use of some NTBs—such as orderly marketing and safeguard (escape clause) actions—and contributed to the reluctance of workers to accept tariff reductions in trade-impacted industries without an improved adjustment assistance program.

The Trade Act of 1974, which authorized U.S. participation in the Tokyo Round, provided for broader adjustment assistance benefits and more realistic eligibility requirements. Programs administered by the Economic Development Administration and other agencies designed to assist restructuring firms grew but, as is discussed in Chapter 3, they did not expand to the point necessary to have a major effect on trade-impacted industries. Programs assisting displaced workers were more extensive, but serious questions have been raised about how effectively they promote structural adjustment and ease long-term burdens on trade-displaced workers.

THE RESULTING TARIFF STRUCTURE

From 1948 to 1962, the no-injury approach to tariff negotiations had a significant effect on the progress of trade liberalization. Under the Reciprocal Trade Agreements Program, the average tariff on dutiable imports fell from 53 percent in 1934 to 12.8 percent in 1952. But as a result of rising protectionist sentiment and concern that tariffs had been cut about as far as possible without causing injury to domestic industries, tariffs declined only slightly over the next decade, to 12.3 percent in 1962.[8] The passage by Congress of the Trade Expansion Act of 1962 authorized the United States to renew its efforts in this area by participating in the Kennedy Round (1964–67),[9] which resulted in a lowering of tariffs by 35 percent in stages from 1968 to 1972.

Further, the policy of reducing tariffs only when danger of injury to the domestic industry could be avoided resulted in a tariff structure that afforded much higher protection to industries most vulnerable to import competition.

Table 1-1 presents the average tariffs levied on all (dutiable and nondutiable) imports across the 17 major (two-digit SIC) sectors included in the Tokyo Round negotiations. These sectors include all manufactured goods except processed food, tobacco and petroleum products. They are ranked by value-added per employee (column 2), from highest to lowest. Higher value-added per employee industries are generally believed to be more intense in the use of R&D and physical capital, as well as highly skilled labor. Further, they are generally believed to produce less standardized products that are not as easily exported by the NICs. In contrast, low value-added per employee industries are generally believed to be more intense in the use of less skilled labor, employ less capital and produce standardized products that are more vulnerable to import competition. The 1966 average tariffs in column 3 may be taken as indicative of the tariffs in place during the Kennedy Round negotiations and just prior to the Kennedy Round tariff cuts. Likewise, the 1976 average tariffs in column 4 are indicative of the tariffs that prevailed after the Kennedy Round cuts and during the Tokyo Round negotiations (1973-79). Column 5 presents estimates of the tariff rates that will prevail after the Tokyo Round cuts are completed. Average tariffs were lowered from 8.7 percent in 1966 to 5.6 percent in 1976, largely as a result of the Kennedy Round. The Tokyo Round will likely reduce average tariffs to less than 4 percent by 1987.

These industries have been divided into quartiles in Table 1-2 according to their value-added per employee. It shows average tariffs for those industries with the highest value-added per employee (Quartile I) to the lowest (Quartile IV).

The principal conclusion emerging from these data is that tariffs tend to be higher in industries that intensively use less skilled labor, employ less capital and produce more standardized products. In 1976, average tariffs for Quartile I were 3.4 percent,

TABLE 1-1. AVERAGE *AD VALOREM* U.S. TARIFFS BY MAJOR SIC SECTOR, 1966, 1976 AND ESTIMATED POST-TOKYO ROUND

Major Manufacturing Sector (SIC)	Value-Added per Employee ($ Thousands)	1966	1976	Estimated Post-Tokyo Round
Chemicals and allied products (28)	$60.39	12.2%	5.2%	3.3%
Paper and allied products (26)	33.51	0.5	0.5	0.2
Transportation equipment (37)	33.38	5.0	1.8	1.4
Instruments and related products (38)	31.63	24.3	9.6	4.9
Primary metal products (33)	30.91	4.9	3.8	2.4
Machinery (exc. electrical) (35)	29.27	8.3	4.4	2.9
Stone, clay and glass products (32)	28.00	21.0	10.8	7.7
Fabricated metal products (34)	26.60	12.4	5.7	3.7
Electric and electronic equipment (36)	26.45	11.6	3.7	2.5
Printing and publishing (27)	25.46	4.1	1.5	0.9
Rubber and miscellaneous plastic products (30)	25.42	14.1	9.0	4.9
Miscellaneous manufactured products (39)	21.52	18.8	8.7	4.9
Lumber and wood products (24)	21.40	5.8	3.6	1.7
Furniture and fixtures (25)	17.32	10.9	4.4	2.2
Textile mill products (22)	16.55	16.5	19.4	12.4
Leather and leather products (31)	14.40	14.5	10.2	9.3
Apparel and other textile products (23)	13.27	22.7	24.5	20.0

Sources: Value-added per employee estimated with data from U.S. Department of Commerce, *Survey of Manufactures, 1976*; 1966 and 1976 tariffs estimated with data from the Department of Labor. Post-Tokyo Round tariffs estimated with data from Alan V. Deardorf and Robert M. Stern, *An Economic Analysis of the Effects of the Multilateral Trade Negotiations on the United States and Other Major Industrialized Countries* (Washington: U.S. Congress, Senate Finance Committee, June 1979), Table 10, p. 43.

TABLE 1-2. AVERAGE *AD VALOREM* U.S. TARIFFS: QUARTILES RANKED BY VALUE-ADDED PER EMPLOYEE, 1966, 1976 AND ESTIMATED POST-TOKYO ROUND
(Percent)

Quartile[1]	1966	1976	Estimated Post-Tokyo Round[2]
I	4.9	3.4	2.2
II	7.1	4.5	2.8
III	10.4	4.7	3.1
IV	14.8	13.7	9.5
Average	8.7	5.6	3.8

1 This category includes industries in Table 1-1 ranked by value-added per employee and divided into four equal groups by value of imports.
2 Estimated post-Tokyo Round tariffs are grouped using 1976 import data.
Source: Authors' estimates.

compared to 4.5, 4.7 and 13.7 percent in Quartiles II, III and IV, respectively. Similar patterns prevailed in 1966 and are likely to continue after the Tokyo Round tariff cuts are implemented.

NONTARIFF BARRIERS

Of course, tariffs are only part of the story. The United States, like other countries, has used various NTBs to protect or encourage adjustment in some trade-impacted industries and to promote exports. When reviewing nontariff practices of any country, it is important to look at those affecting both imports and exports to obtain a balanced view. Both types of policies impact trade patterns, the structure of domestic industry, employment and income levels, balance of payments, and exchange rates. U.S. measures affecting imports include those restricting imports of specific products where sudden import surges have disrupted domestic markets. In most cases, these measures are temporary and intended to provide "breathing room" for adjustment or to overcome periods of slack demand. At various times in recent years, the United States has negotiated orderly marketing agreements (OMAs) for carbon steel, specialty steel, textiles and apparel, nonrubber footwear, and color televisions. And, for three years beginning in 1981, Japan has agreed to limit shipments of automobiles to the United States. Other imports have also been subject to additional tariffs or quantitative restrictions under safeguard actions.

Other trade measures have protected a wider scope of industries and are more permanent.[10] These include various aspects of U.S. customs valuation and invoicing procedures, federal, state and local government procurement practices, and certain aspects of U.S. product standards.

Furthermore, the U.S. government has provided various direct and indirect subsidies to ease structural adjustment or maintain employment in import-impacted industries, such as textiles and footwear, and to achieve other economic and social goals, such as the development of depressed regions. Like subsidies in other industrial countries, these subsidies may displace imports and increase exports but, as discussed in Chapter 3, U.S. efforts in this area are small.

Finally, the United States has sought to meet the competition from other industrial countries in export financing, and extends much bilateral aid on a tied basis but, as discussed in Chapter 4, its efforts in this area are also relatively modest.

As the "Introduction" stated, the primary purposes of this study are to describe these practices, to provide initial estimates of the tariff equivalent effects of these NTBs on industrial imports, and to give some indication of the effects on these practices of the recently negotiated GATT codes[11] and the tax and spending policies implemented by the Reagan Administration. In this way, a first approximation is offered of the importance of nontariff impediments to imports relative to tariffs and natural barriers in the United States.

Table 1-3 summarizes the estimates of the average protection from tariffs, the additional protection offered by measures limiting imports and promoting domestic production and exports, as well as that afforded producers by natural protective barriers to trade (e.g., transportation costs).

Again as noted in the "Introduction," many assumptions were necessary to estimate the tariff equivalents of the protection provided by various U.S. NTBs; therefore, these estimates should be viewed as only approximate measures and some as order of magnitude estimates. Further, it was not possible to measure the effects of several important NTBs that limit imports, most significantly the effects of some product standards and state and local government procurement practices. Nevertheless, the data in Table 1-3 provide a good first indication of the relative importance of U.S. import barriers and export promotion programs. These data indicate that, on average over the full range of manufactured products, the protection given by NTBs that may limit or reduce imports[12] (about 2 percent) is not nearly as large as the protection afforded by tariffs (about 5 percent) or natural barriers to trade (about 4 per-

TABLE 1-3. SUMMARY FINDINGS: ESTIMATED TARIFF AND SUBSIDY EQUIVALENTS OF U.S. INDUSTRIAL TRADE-DISTORTING PRACTICES, 1976

Tariffs (c.i.f.)*	4.93%
NTBs affecting producer and consumer prices (quantitative restrictions and safeguards, customs valuation, discriminatory excise taxes, and federal government procurement)	1.07
Domestic production subsidies (below-market credit, technical assistance, tax incentives, and benefits-in-kind)	0.94
Export subsidies (below-market export credits, DISCs, OPIC, tied aid, others)	2.76
Total imposed protection[1]	6.71
Natural rate of protection[2]	4.14
Total protection[1]	10.55

*Cost, insurance, freight.
1 These are not simple sums. The methodology is explained in Tables 5-1 and 5-2.
2 The natural rate of protection is the cost of transporting goods from the exporting country to the importing country (freight, insurance and so on) divided by the value of imports.
Source: Authors' estimates.

cent). Like tariffs, they offer important amounts of protection to selected industries, but, overall, they do not appear to be any more important than tariffs. Also, like tariffs, the protection received from several practices will decline with the implementation of the GATT codes and President Reagan's economic program. Further, the subsidies implicit in programs that encourage exports[13] (about 4 percent) do not appear to be as great as the protection provided import-competing industries by tariffs and NTBs (about 7 percent).[14]

Notes

1 That is, externalities, less than competitive conditions and other market distortions.

2 Also, in the absence of externalities, the cost faced by producers would just equal the full costs to society of the resources employed.

3 Government spending and regulatory policies designed to redress this imbalance—such as government funding for certain types of R&D or environmental regulations—are not TDPs under this definition.

4 For example, the United States encouraged the formation of the European Community as part of U.S. efforts to strengthen the West European economy. By eliminating tariffs among its member states, the EC increased inter-European trade but reduced U.S. exports to Europe; for an analysis see Lawrence B. Krause, *European Economic Integration and the United States* (Washington: Brookings Institution, 1968). In another example, Canada, the U.S.'s largest trading partner, did not participate fully in the item-by-item tariff reductions negotiated in the Kennedy Round. As a result, Canada's post-Kennedy Round tariffs were, on average, higher than U.S. tariffs. The Office of the U.S. Trade Representative estimated that prior to the Tokyo Round, the average Canadian tariff on dutiable U.S. imports was about 14.8 percent, while the average U.S. tariff on dutiable Canadian imports was 5.2 percent. These rates are expected to fall to 8.5 and 2.8 percent after the Tokyo Round tariff reductions are completed. Further, a larger share of Canada's exports enter the United States duty free (about 70 percent) than the share of U.S. exports entering Canada duty free (about 40 percent). See Office of the U.S. Trade Representative, *Results of the United States Industrial Tariff Negotiations with Other Major Developed Countries in the Multilateral Trade Negotiations* (Washington, June 21, 1979, mimeo).

5 Harold J. Clem, *United States International Economic Policy* (Washington: Industrial College of the Armed Forces, 1976), pp. 26-27.

6 Ibid., p. 28.

7 Ibid., p. 76.

8 Ibid., p. 35.

9 Ibid.

10 The use of these practices will be limited by the recently implemented GATT codes governing the use of NTBs. The codes cover government procurement, subsidies and countervailing duties, standards, import licensing, customs valuation, and safeguards.

11 See footnote 10.

12 These are NTBs that affect producer and consumer prices and domestic production subsidies.

13 These include domestic production subsidies and export subsidies.

14 In evaluating these results, the reader may wish to consider two additional points. First, over the past two or three years, high U.S. interest rates have contributed to the strength of the dollar on international markets. To the extent that the dollar appreciated by more than can be justified by changes in U.S. costs of production, as compared with those of major U.S. competitors, the resulting overvaluation of the dollar reduces the protection afforded U.S. import-competing and export industries provided by the NTBs discussed here.

Second, the estimates presented in Table 1-3 are averages. Since the benefits provided by many NTBs are often highly focused, it is important to keep in mind that they give significant levels of protection to selected firms and industries.

TDPs Affecting Producer and Consumer Prices 2

At various times, the United States has imposed restrictions on imports, negotiated restraints on exports and adopted administrative practices that reduce imports. To some degree, such practices insulate domestic producers from foreign competition and may lead to higher prices for consumers.[1]

First, some of these NTBs were designed to limit market disruptions and threats to the viability of domestic industries created by sudden and large import surges. These include orderly marketing agreements negotiated with principal exporting countries, quotas and additional duties imposed under GATT Article XIX safeguard actions. These measures have usually been temporary, although the protection afforded the textile and apparel industries (via the Multi-Fiber Arrangement) has become more or less permanent.

Second, other NTBs have been in place for many years but will become less effective or even end as the GATT codes governing NTBs are implemented. Some of these were put in place, or made more restrictive, as a result of periodic increases in protectionist sentiment, while others were created to shield some industries from the adverse effects of changes in U.S. laws governing trade. These include federal, state and local procurement practices and various aspects of U.S. customs valuation and invoicing procedures. In contrast, other long-standing NTBs evolved by accident, the outgrowth of domestic policies not intended to restrict imports. These include some product standards that make exporting to the United States difficult.

QUANTITATIVE RESTRICTIONS

As tariffs have declined, quantitative restrictions have become an attractive alternative for limiting imports that disrupt domestic markets or threaten employment. While GATT signator countries are generally not permitted to impose quotas on industrial imports,[2] the GATT permits exceptions under the safeguard or escape clause (Article XIX). As discussed below, countries may impose *temporary* quotas and additional duties to protect domestic industries.

Alternatively, signator countries have been able to limit imports through OMAs or voluntary export restraints (VERs) negotiated formally or informally with the principal exporting countries. Under these arrangements, exporting countries will agree to limit shipments to avoid stronger measures that may ultimately be imposed under a safeguard action. In recent years, such measures have been the principal means used by the United States to place quantitative limits on industrial imports, and safeguard actions have been used almost exclusively to impose additional duties.[3] This section reviews the agreements limiting imports obtained by the United States and examines policies in two other sectors that also reduce imports. The next section reviews U.S. safeguard actions taken under Article XIX.[4]

Since 1975, the United States has negotiated OMAs to limit imports of nonrubber footwear, color televisions, specialty steel, and textiles and apparel. The important features of these agreements are summarized in Table 2-1. Also, in 1981, Japan agreed to limit automobile exports to the United States for three years. Further, under a provision of the Manufacturing Clause of the U.S. Copyright Law that predates the GATT Articles of Agreement, imports of nondramatic literary publications authored by U.S. residents but published outside the United States are discouraged.

(1) Nonrubber Footwear

The nonrubber footwear industry is typical of mature manufacturing industries in the AICs that are vulnerable to competition from NIC exports. It is intense in the use of less skilled labor and employs standardized technologies. Furthermore, the industry is particularly vulnerable to competition because small-scale facilities employing little capital can be internationally competitive in low wage countries. For example, in 1979, Taiwan had 582 factories with only 94,000 workers—162 employees per fac-

TABLE 2-1. MAJOR U.S. QUANTITATIVE RESTRICTIONS OF INDUSTRIAL IMPORTS, 1975-81

Product	Dates	Type of Restriction	Affected Countries	Estimated Tariff Equivalent	Assumed Elasticity[1]	Imports ($ Millions)	Four-Digit SIC Classification
Nonrubber footwear	6/28/77–6/30/81	OMAs	Taiwan, S. Korea	1977 2.1% 1978 2.1 1979 1.5 1977-79 1.9	4.07	1976 $1092.6 1977 1177.4 1978 1972.6 1979 2317.4	314: 3142-House slippers 3143-Men's except athletic 3144-Women's except athletic 3149-Footwear, except rubber, nec.*
Color televisions	7/1/77–6/30/80 (Japan) 2/1/79–6/30/82 (Taiwan and S. Korea)	OMAs	Japan, Taiwan, S. Korea	1978 0.4–0.7% 1979 6.7–13.4	2.8	1976 967.5 1977 973.5 1978 1334.9 1979 1182.3	pt 3651-Radio and TV receiving sets, except communication types
Specialty steel	6/76–2/13/80	OMAs–Japan; Quotas–others	Japan, EC, Sweden, Canada, and others	6/76–6/79 6%[2] 7/79–2/81 n.e.	n.a.	1975 $194.6 1976 213.2 1977 210.7 1978 250.8	pt 3312-Blast furnaces (including coke ovens), steel works and rolling mills
Textiles and apparel	1973-81	Multi-Fiber Arrangement allows bilateral agreements	Hong Kong, Japan, S. Korea, Taiwan, and others	Textiles n.e. Apparel 8.8%	n.a. 3.66	1976 $4883 1977 5415 1978 7045 1979 7229 1980 8180 1981 9506	22-Textile mill products 23-Apparel and other finished products made from fabrics and similar materials
Automobiles	4/81–3/84	Japan has agreed to limit shipments	Japan	2.5	2.4	1980 16,675.2 1981 17,964.7	3711-Motor vehicles and passenger car bodies
Book printing and publishing	1891–	Imports implicitly discouraged	All, but Far East affected most	31.2–42.4%	1.4	1976 $161.5 1977 171.8 1978 238.2 1979 272.2 1980 306.8 1981 300.0	2731-32

* not elsewhere classified.
n.e. = not estimable.
n.a. = not available.
1 Assumed import elasticity is reported when employed to estimate the tariff equivalent. In these cases, the percent change in imports induced by the quantitative restriction was divided by the elasticity to obtain the estimated tariff equivalent.
2 Estimate for stainless sheet and strip steel (imports of which accounted for 48.8 percent of total specialty steel imports from 7/76–6/79) for 1976-77 quota year. We believe this provides a reasonable estimate for the first three quota years.
Sources: Columns 2, 4: Presidential Proclamations 4510 and 4769 (Washington, 1977 and 1980); International Trade Commission; U.S. Department of Agriculture; and U.S. Department of Labor. Column 7: ITC Publication Nos. 968 (1979), 1068 (1980) and 1329 (1982); Department of Labor; Department of Commerce, *U.S. Industrial Outlook*, various issues.

tory. Approximately half these establishments had fewer than 100 employees and were capitalized at less than $83,000.[5]

From 1971 to 1976, U.S. production of footwear fell 21 percent, while the import share of the U.S. market (measured in pairs of shoes) grew from 33 percent to 47 percent. Taiwan and South Korea led the import surge, capturing 25 percent of the U.S. market in 1976 (see Table 2-2).

Faced with continuing plant closures and declining employment, the industry petitioned the International Trade Commission (ITC) for a safeguard investigation in September 1975. The process was halted after OMAs negotiated with Taiwan and Korea became effective June 28, 1977. The OMAs lasted four years and were terminated on June 30, 1981. In 1976, Taiwan and Korea exported to the United States 156 and 44 million pairs of shoes, respectively. OMAs set the following limits on their exports to the United States, in millions of pairs:

	Taiwan	S. Korea
1977–78	122	33.0
1978–79	125	36.5
1979–80	128	37.5
1980–81	131	38.0

The OMAs did curtail the volume of imports from Taiwan and Korea, but the domestic footwear industry did not reap the full benefits for two reasons. First, from 1976 to 1979, imports from Taiwan and Korea declined by 50 million pairs, but imports from other sources increased by 85 million pairs. This surge was caused by several factors.

TABLE 2-2. U.S. NONRUBBER FOOTWEAR MARKET, 1971 AND 1974–80

	1971	1974	1975	1976	1977	1978	1979	1980
				(Millions of Pairs)				
Apparent consumption	818.6	715.5	702.4	788.9	793.6	779.5	797.9	740.6
Imported supply	268.6	266.4	287.8	370.0	368.1	373.5	404.6	365.7
Taiwan	—	88.3	103.4	155.7	166.5	117.2	124.9	144.0
S. Korea	—	9.2	16.0	44.0	58.7	30.6	24.4	37.0
Uncontrolled	—	168.9	168.4	170.3	142.9	225.7	255.3	184.7
				Import Share of U.S. Market				
				(Percent)				
All imports	32.8	37.2	41.0	46.9	46.4	47.9	50.7	49.4
Taiwan	—	12.3	14.7	19.7	21.0	15.0	15.6	19.5
S. Korea	—	1.3	2.3	5.6	7.4	3.9	3.1	5.0
Uncontrolled	—	23.6	24.0	21.6	18.2	29.0	32.0	24.9

Sources: ITC, *Nonrubber Footwear*, ITC Publication No. 1139 (Washington, April 1981); *Nonrubber Footwear: U.S. Production, Exports, Imports for Consumption . . . Second Calendar Quarter 1980*, ITC Publication No. 1091 (August 1980); *Footwear*, ITC Publication No. 799 (February 1977).

- The manufacture of inexpensive footwear is easily established and expanded in other NICs because of its low skill and capital requirements—after the OMAs were put in place, imports from Brazil, Hong Kong, the Philippines, Mexico, and Singapore increased substantially.

- Taiwanese producers established factories assembling components in Hong Kong and Singapore.

- From 1977 to 1979, U.S. imports of Italian shoes jumped dramatically, accounting for 51 percent of the increase in uncontrolled imports, as a result of a temporary fashion fad for Candie shoes (see Table 2-3).

Second (and just as significant to domestic producers), from 1976 to 1979, the unit value of imported footwear increased by about 55 percent, while domestic producer prices increased about 29 percent. Their exports thus constrained in volume terms, Taiwan and Korea began competing, to a limited degree, with U.S. producers in somewhat higher priced lines. While the volume of their shipments to the United States declined 25 percent, the value of their shipments increased 14 percent. This had adverse consequences for U.S. firms and workers producing higher priced, higher quality shoes.

In 1980, Taiwan and Korea regained much of their lost market share because:

- U.S. demand for shoes fell by 7 percent from 1979 and, in a contracting market, Taiwanese and Korean producers were better able to maintain—in fact, to increase slightly—their sales than were other foreign producers. Taiwanese and Korean producers seem to continue to be the most efficient foreign suppliers of inexpensive footwear.

- The bottom fell out of the demand for Italian Candie shoes and, in 1980, Italian exports to the United States fell by 52 percent from 1979 levels.

- Taiwanese producers reduced their activities in Hong Kong as a result of certificate-of-origin requirements imposed by the United States in 1978 and were ordered out of Singapore by its government in 1979.

TABLE 2-3. U.S. NONRUBBER FOOTWEAR IMPORTS, 1977-80

	1977	1978	1979	1980	Percent Change 1977-80
	(Thousands of Pairs)				
Total imports	368,069	373,518	404,563	365,743	− 1
Taiwan	166,478	117,235	124,865	144,032	− 13
S. Korea	58,650	30,591	24,388	37,054	− 37
Other NICs*	34,502	76,195	85,257	83,134	+ 141
Italy	39,674	62,934	97,074	46,221	+ 17
All others	68,765	86,563	72,979	55,302	− 20

*These are Brazil, Hong Kong, the Philippines, Mexico, Thailand, Singapore, India, and China.
Source: ITC, *Nonrubber Footwear*, ITC Publication No. 1139 (Washington, April 1981).

As a result, Taiwan and Korea's share of the U.S. market stood at 25 percent in 1980, just 1 percentage point less than in 1976. The overall import share of the market was 49 percent in 1980, up from 47 percent in 1976.

Therefore, over the entire 1976 to 1980 period, the OMAs did constrain imports from Taiwan and Korea but also encouraged the development of new sources of supply in other NICs. The lack of restraints on imports from these sources, as well as Italy, limited the effectiveness of the OMAs.

In 1982, the ITC published an econometric analysis of the impact of the OMAs on U.S. imports over the 1977-79 period.[6]

	Actual Imports	Estimated Reduction in Imports	Estimated Reduction in Imports
	(Millions of Pairs)		(Percent)
1977	368.1	−31.84	7.96
1978	373.5	−31.33	7.74
1979	404.6	−24.75	5.77
Total	1,146.2	−87.92	7.12

Applying the methodology described in Appendix C, and assuming the import demand elasticity for nonrubber footwear to be 4.1,[7] the estimated tariff that would have had the equivalent impact on imports over the 1977-79 period is 1.9 percent. This represents protection over and above that provided by the post-Kennedy Round tariff on nonrubber footwear, which averaged 9.2 percent.[8]

(2) Color Televisions

During the mid-1970s, the competitive position of the U.S. color television industry eroded substantially. From 1971 to 1974, imports' share of domestic purchases of complete television sets (measured in number of sets), fluctuated around 16 percent, increased in 1975 to 18 percent, and rose in 1976 to 33 percent. Japan accounted for about 85 percent of these sales.

In an effort to avoid a strong U.S. safeguard action, Japan agreed to an OMA on its exports of *complete* and *incomplete* color televisions. The OMA limited the volume of exports in each of these two categories to about 70 percent of 1976 levels for three years effective July 1, 1977.

As a result of constraints on Japanese producers, imports from Taiwan and South Korea increased fourfold. From 1976 to 1978, the Japanese import share of the domestic market declined 30 percent to 14 percent but, overall, the import share declined from 33 percent to only 26 percent. As a result, OMAs were negotiated with Taiwan and Korea (effective from February 1, 1979 through June 30, 1980), also restricting imports of complete and incomplete sets.

During the three years Japanese imports were constrained, four major Japanese producers established plants in the United States, joining three other companies. The quotas for complete Japanese color receivers were *not* filled for any of the OMA years. By 1979, the volume of Japanese imports of complete receivers was only one-quarter of the 1976 level. However, imports of components for assembly in the United States—incomplete sets and subassemblies—increased significantly. From 1976 to 1979, the value of imports from all sources of incomplete sets for assembly in the United States increased over 300 percent. During the first six months of Japan's last OMA year, 82 percent of its quota for incomplete sets was filled. Further, from 1976 to 1979, the value of imports of subassemblies, which were not covered by the OMAs, doubled.

As a result of the decline in Japan's exports to the United States and the location of Japanese production facilities here, Japan's OMA was permitted to expire on schedule. Taiwan's and Korea's OMAs were extended two more years and then expired.

Although the OMAs achieved some of their intended purpose, especially in terms of trade with Japan, evidence indicates that, like footwear, the OMAs' impact was limited, first because of shifts in the source of imports and second because of changes in the composition of imports.

For 1976, 1978 and 1979, Table 2-4 presents imported complete and incomplete sets' share of domestic consumption and imported subassemblies' share of domestic shipments. The last full year without an OMA was 1976, and 1979 was the first year in which OMAs constrained imports from Japan, Taiwan and Korea. The data are presented in value terms so that information for sets at various stages of completion may be compared.

After the OMA was put in place on imports of complete and incomplete sets from Japan, the Japanese market share declined from 18.7 percent in 1976 to 10.8 in 1978. Meanwhile, the market share captured by imports from Taiwan and Korea jumped from 1.5 to 7.2 percent. Therefore, the market share filled by imports from all sources declined only marginally, from 21.3 in 1976 to 20.9 percent in 1978. After

TABLE 2-4. CONSUMPTION AND IMPORTS OF COMPLETE AND INCOMPLETE COLOR TELEVISIONS, 1976, 1978 AND 1979
($ Thousands and Percent)

	1976	1978	1979
Apparent consumption	$2593	$3245	$3340
Import share	21.3%	20.9%	13.7%
Complete sets	19.4	17.1	8.8
Japan	17.8	9.8	3.9
Taiwan and S. Korea	1.5	5.7	3.7
Others	0.2	1.6	1.2
Incomplete sets*	1.9	3.8	4.9
Japan	0.9	1.0	1.1
Taiwan and S. Korea	—	1.5	1.1
Others	1.0	1.3	2.7
Addendum			
Subassembly imports divided by industry shipments	13.2%	17.5%	18.3%

*Complete color televisions constitute a clearly definable entity. Incomplete color televisions are less easily specified. However, in general, an incomplete receiver is one that is substantially assembled, consisting of a picture tube packaged with a significant portion of the other electronics or chassis.
Source: ITC, *Color Televisions and Subassemblies Thereof*, ITC Publication No. 1068 (Washington, May 1980).

imports from Japan, Korea and Taiwan were constrained in 1979, the import market share declined to 13.7 percent.

As the Japanese producers replaced their exports with sets produced in U.S. factories, imports of subassemblies increased substantially, from 13.2 percent of U.S. shipments in 1976 to 18.3 percent in 1979. Nevertheless, this shift of imports from completed and incomplete sets to components for assembly greatly increased value-added in the United States.

An answer to a difficult but key question is important in evaluating the impacts of the OMAs for color TV: to what extent was the 36 percent reduction in the import share of the U.S. market for complete and incomplete sets from 1976 to 1979 caused by the OMAs and to what extent was it caused by the movement of Japanese producers to the United States that would have taken place without the OMAs? Some Japanese producers came to the United States before the OMAs, but there is really no sure way to discern the motives of Japanese producers who came afterward.

In the absence of a satisfactory econometric analysis for the 1976 to 1979 period, a range of values for the OMAs' impacts on imports may be selected to estimate a range for the tariff equivalent. If the entire decline in the import market share is attributed to the OMAs, then in 1979 the OMAs had a restraining effect on imports equivalent to a 13.4 percent tariff.[9] If only half the decline is attributed to the OMAs, the comparable tariff would be 6.7 percent. These estimates are reported in Table 2-1, as an estimated range of the impact of the OMAs in 1979, and similar computations were made for 1978. This is protection over and above the 5 percent average tariff that was in place.

(3) Carbon Steel and Specialty Steel

Carbon Steel

From 1969 to 1974, Japan and the European Coal and Steel Community voluntarily limited exports of certain mill fabricated products to the United States, as did the United Kingdom from 1972 to 1974. By 1973, U.S. mills were at full capacity, and in 1974, these agreements were allowed to expire.

In 1977, however, carbon steel imports surged from 14.4 percent in 1976 to 17.8 percent of U.S. apparent consumption. American steel company profits dropped to 2 percent of 1976 levels, and many steel mills either shut down or operated at sharply curtailed levels. Meanwhile, 19 antidumping complaints had been filed with the Treasury Department; one had already been determined affirmatively, and it appeared that many of the others would also be determined affirmatively. A solution was needed that would be sensitive both to the political relationships involved and to the economic reality faced by the domestic producers. The Solomon Task Force, established to study the industry and its problems, recommended the implementation of a trigger price system to protect the U.S. steel industry from the sale of foreign steel products at less than fair value—i.e., at less than production costs.

The Carter Administration put the trigger price mechanism (TPM) in place early in 1978. So-called trigger prices were established for each type of steel based on production costs of the most efficient producers in Japan, plus transportation costs.[10] To the extent that the TPM functioned as intended and Japanese production costs were accurately estimated, the TPM operated as an automatic antidumping mechanism designed to protect American producers from unfair competition, as opposed to a trade-distorting practice.

In March 1980, the TPM was suspended when U.S. Steel accused European producers of dumping in a case filed with the International Trade Commission. In October 1980, the TPM was reinstated when U.S. Steel agreed to withdraw its complaint in return for a strengthened TPM. The Commerce Department itself initiated dumping investigations in November 1981 against hot-rolled carbon steel plate from Belgium, Brazil, Rumania, and South Africa; hot-rolled carbon steel sheet from France; sheet piling from Canada; and structural steel from Spain.

In January 1982, domestic steel producers filed petitions with the ITC and the Commerce Department claiming that certain steel imports from Belgium, France, Italy, Luxembourg, the Netherlands, Rumania, the United Kingdom, and West Germany were government subsidized and/or were being sold in the United States at less than full value (which is dumping). The TPM was suspended again while the U.S. government investigated. In August 1982, the Commerce Department found steel imports from West Germany, Belgium, France, Italy, Luxembourg, and the United Kingdom subsidized. Further, in a preliminary ruling the Commerce Department found five West European nations and Rumania to be dumping. The ITC, whose task it is to determine injury, rejected cases pertaining to some steel products from West Germany but ruled that the U.S. industry had indeed been injured by imports from Belgium, France, Italy, Luxembourg, and some from Germany. Penalties in the form of additional duties ranging from less than 1 percent to about 26 percent of the value of imports were to be imposed on various types of steel from those countries.

Shortly before the imposition of these penalties in October 1982, the Common Market agreed to limit European steel exports from November 1, 1982 to the end of 1985. Shipments of carbon and alloy steel will be limited to about 5.5 percent of projected U.S. apparent consumption.[11] In 1981, imports of these products from the EC accounted for about 5.9 percent of the U.S. market. EC imports of pipe and tube products, which were not the object of countervailing or antidumping suits, will also be limited to 5.9 percent compared to 6.2 percent in 1981.

If the United States had imposed countervailing duties to offset the effects of EC subsidies and dumping, these duties would not be construed as trade-distorting practices by the definition offered in Chapter 1. When faced with countervailing duties designed to offset the effects of their subsidies and dumping, the EC apparently found the limitations on exports to the United States described above less restrictive overall (even though they covered a wider range of products). In this light, these restrictions may be viewed as substitutes for nontrade-distorting countervailing duties.

Specialty Steel

After the voluntary restraints on Japanese and European steel expired in 1974, U.S. producers of specialty steel (stainless and alloy steel), who account for 1 percent of total U.S. steel production, continued to be adversely affected by imports. The import share of domestic consumption increased from 11.4 percent in 1974 to 18.1 percent in 1975 as capacity utilization fell from 74 percent in 1973 and 86 percent in 1974 to only 48 percent in 1975.

Domestic producers petitioned the ITC for relief, and the ITC recommended quantitative restrictions on some categories of specialty steel. Before granting this relief, the President tried to negotiate OMAs with the leading exporting nations. Japan agreed to a three-year OMA beginning June 14, 1976, which set annual limits on imports for five categories of specialty steel—stainless sheet and strip, stainless plate, stainless bars, stainless rods, and alloy tool steel. The agreement was extended eight months and terminated February 13, 1980. Safeguard (Article XIX) quotas were imposed on imports from other countries.

Stainless sheet and strip was the largest category covered by the OMA and quotas, accounting for about two-thirds of domestic production from 1976 to 1979. An econometric analysis undertaken for the ITC estimated that during the 1976-77 quota years, the price of foreign stainless sheet and strip steel would have had to rise by 6 percent to reduce imports as much as the import restrictions did.[12] This is the figure reported in Table 2-1 as the tariff equivalent of the OMAs on specialty steel.

Specialty steel was not covered by the trigger price mechanism but, since January 1981, the Commerce Department has monitored specialty steel imports. The purpose is to ensure quick application of U.S. trade laws if specialty steel imports should surge as a result of dumping or foreign government subsidies.

(4) Textiles and Apparel

The textile and apparel industries also have a long history of protection. The first internationally sanctioned arrangement was a one-year agreement on cotton textiles and apparel concluded in 1961 at a meeting called by the GATT at the request of the United States. This was followed in 1962 by a long-term arrangement on cotton that ran initially for five years and was extended for three-year periods in 1967 and 1970.

The agreement allowed participating GATT countries to limit imports of cotton textiles or cotton goods that were disrupting or threatening to disrupt domestic markets. Exporting countries were asked to limit their shipments; if this was not done, importers could limit imports to the levels of the preceding year. Under the agreement, the United States had arrangements with 27 exporting nations, accounting for 90 percent of U.S. cotton textile and apparel imports.

In 1973, an Arrangement Regarding International Trade in Textiles (more commonly known as the Multi-Fiber Arrangement) was negotiated covering manmade fibers and wool in addition to cotton textiles and apparel. The MFA went into effect for four years, beginning January 1, 1974, and has been extended twice, with the current agreement expiring on July 31, 1986.

The United States controls textile and apparel imports through bilateral agreements negotiated within the framework of the MFA. As of November 1, 1982, the United States has agreements with 24 countries specifically limiting imports[13] and agreements with 10 other countries providing for possible limitations if problems arise. During 1976-79, the countries with which bilateral agreements were in force accounted for about 80 percent of all cotton, wool and manmade fiber textiles imported into the United States. Under the MFA, the United States agrees to allow restricted imports to grow a minimum of 6 percent a year, but exceptions are made for some countries and products.

From 1973 to 1981, domestic textile consumption grew 0.7 and imports 2.6 percent a year. The same figures for apparel consumption and imports were 1.3 and 7.7 percent, respectively.[14] So the United States is allowing imports to grow faster than its domestic market, dramatically in the case of apparel.

It is difficult to measure the restrictive effects of the MFA because textile and apparel imports have been controlled to some extent for two decades. There is no period to use as a basis for comparison of past and present import penetration. However, it is possible to construct an hypothesis about how much imports would have grown without the MFA to obtain an estimate of the order of magnitude of the MFA's restrictive effects.

For apparel, a set of assumptions was selected that could yield a conservative estimate of the growth in imports that would have taken place in the absence of the MFA.

First, it was assumed that, from 1973 to 1978, imports would have absorbed all the growth in apparel consumption. In other words, it was assumed that without the MFA, imports in a typical or average year would have increased as much as the inflation-adjusted value of domestic sales and that domestic producers would have continued to sell the same volume of products. This seems like a reasonable assumption of what could have taken place, considering that prior to 1978 domestic production in the nonrubber footwear industry declined steadily without long-term protection. The years 1973 and 1978 were selected because 1973 was the last year before the MFA went into effect, and 1973 and 1978 were the peak years for apparel consumption over the last full business cycle (1973-79).

Second, it was assumed that if the MFA were removed, foreign suppliers would only be able to recapture three years of lost import growth in any single typical year. If the MFA were removed and the only barriers to imports were existing tariffs, it is extremely unlikely that foreign suppliers could quickly make up for 20 years of lost import growth. Yet, imports would certainly grow faster on an annual basis than they would have if import restrictions had not been in place in the past. Foreign suppliers' achieving three-years' growth in one year would impose considerable disruptions on domestic producers.

Using the first assumption, a time series for hypothetical imports may be generated and compared with actual imports for 1973 to 1978. This is illustrated in Table 2-5, where under this assumption, hypothetical imports are 43.6 percent larger than actual imports by 1978. Applying the second assumption, removing agreements negotiated under the MFA would increase imports by about 26.2 percent in one year. A tariff that would constrain imports by the same amount would be about 8.8 percent.[15] This estimated protection is provided by the agreements negotiated under the MFA and is in addition to the considerable tariff protection (23.1 percent c.i.f. and 24.5 percent f.o.b.) provided apparel.

Alternatively, this calculation could have been performed for the growth in imports between 1973 and 1979. These years were the peak years in terms of GNP growth

TABLE 2-5. U.S. APPAREL CONSUMPTION AND IMPORTS, 1973 AND 1977-79
(Millions of 1972 Dollars)

	1973	1977	1978	1979
Apparent consumption	$30,394	$32,933	$34,518	$32,790
Actual imports	2,170	2,771	3,548	3,478
Hypothetical imports[1]	2,170	4,709	6,294	4,566
Percent difference[2]	—	41.2%	43.6%	23.8%

1 Apparent consumption in current year (i.e., 1977, 1978 or 1979) less apparent consumption in 1973 plus imports in 1973.
2 Actual imports less hypothetical imports, divided by hypothetical imports.
Source: Department of Commerce, *U.S. Industrial Outlook* (Washington), various issues.

for the last full major business cycle. For 1979, hypothetical imports were 23.8 percent larger than actual imports. Applying the second assumption, removing the agreements negotiated under the MFA would increase imports by 11.9 percent, and the estimated tariff equivalent would be 4.0 percent.

Evaluating the effects of the agreements negotiated under the MFA for textiles is even more difficult because many branches of U.S. textiles have once again become internationally competitive. New, advanced production techniques and improved management are helping U.S. firms and workers overcome the wage advantage held by many foreign competitors. Particularly important have been investments in new process technologies and improvements in the industry's management capabilities that have made possible significant productivity improvements. Over the 1968–78 period, textiles ranked fifth among the 20 major manufacturing sectors (i.e., two-digit SIC industries) in the growth of output per manhour. By this measure, productivity in the textile sector grew at a 3.8 percent average annual rate, while the average for all manufacturing was only 2.3 percent.[16]

While many textile lines and firms still require the MFA's protection to remain viable, it is difficult to obtain data on them for the kind of analysis just performed for apparel. Production, exports and import data are not available on a consistent basis at a sufficient level of disaggregation to sort out export-competitive and import-competing industries.[17]

In the years ahead, the textile industry may be threatened as much by import competition in the industries that use its products (e.g., apparel and automobiles) as by direct import competition. A declining domestic apparel sector could require the textile industry to expand exports more rapidly than is possible if current employment levels are to be maintained.

(5) Automobiles

U.S. automobile producers entered the 1960s with a dominant position in the North American market, as U.S. and Canadian preferences for large cars provided them with an assured demand. In 1964, total U.S. imports from non-Canadian sources were only about 6.5 percent of U.S. consumption (see Table 2–6); 68 percent of these imports came from West Germany, which enjoyed unchallenged success in the subcompact market with the Volkswagen Beetle. Imports from Canada were negligible, as high tariffs and other protective measures resulted in an inefficient structure of production there. The United States had a surplus in automotive trade with Canada, but most of the vehicles sold in Canada were produced there on short production runs.

During the latter half of the 1960s, U.S. imports began to rise as a result of two quite separate forces. First, in 1965, the United States and Canada entered into the Automotive Agreement, which resulted in virtually duty-free trade between the two countries in cars, trucks and original equipment parts. To ensure that Canada obtained what its government perceived to be a fair share of North American production, it obtained Letters of Undertaking from U.S. auto makers in which they agreed to certain production goals for Canada. The end result of these "safeguards" was to encourage the major automobile manufacturers to locate parts production in the United States and vehicle assembly in Canada. Over the years, the United States has generally had a surplus in its parts trade with Canada and a deficit in its vehicles trade. From 1964 to 1970, vehicle imports from Canada grew from 0.1 percent of U.S. consumption to 8.4 percent. Since that time, the Canadian import market share has fluctuated

TABLE 2-6. DOMESTIC AND IMPORT SHARES OF THE U.S. PASSENGER AUTOMOBILE MARKET, 1964-81

	Factory Sales	Imports	Apparent Consumption	Import Share of Apparent Consumption			
	(1000s of Vehicles)			Total	Canada	Non-Canadian	Japan
1964	7,752	537	8,107	6.6%	0.1%	6.5%	0.2%
1965	9,306	564	9,763	5.8	0.3	5.5	0.3
1966	8,598	900	9,321	9.7	1.6	8.1	0.6
1967	7,437	1,021	8,177	12.5	4.6	7.9	0.9
1968	8,822	1,620	10,112	16.0	5.0	11.0	1.7
1969	8,824	1,847	9,737	19.0	7.1	11.9	2.8
1970	6,547	2,013	8,275	24.3	8.4	13.9	4.6
1971	8,585	2,587	10,785	24.0	7.4	16.6	6.5
1972	8,824	2,486	10,899	22.8	7.7	15.1	6.4
1973	9,658	2,437	11,586	21.0	7.5	13.5	8.5
1974	7,311	2,573	9,283	27.7	8.8	18.9	8.5
1975	7,613	2,075	8,145	25.5	9.0	16.5	8.5
1976	8,498	2,537	10,354	24.5	8.0	16.5	10.9
1977	9,199	2,790	11,292	24.7	7.5	16.2	11.9
1978	9,165	3,001	11,481	26.1	7.3	18.8	13.6
1979	8,419	3,006	10,643	28.2	6.4	21.8	15.2
1980	6,340	3,116	8,904	35.0	6.7	28.3	22.4
1981	6,255	2,856	8,566	33.3	6.6	26.7	23.2

Source: ITC, *The U.S. Auto Industry: U.S. Factory Sales, Retail Sales, Imports, Exports, Apparent Consumption, Suggested Retail Prices and Trade Balances with Selected Countries for Motor Vehicles, 1964-81*, ITC Publication No. 1329 (Washington, December 1982).

between a high of 9.0 percent in 1975 to a low of 6.4 percent in 1979. Today, the U.S. and Canadian industries are fully integrated, and the two countries face the same troubling problems associated with the declining competitiveness of the North American industry.

Second, from the mid-1960s onward, imports from Japan (in particular those produced by Datsun and Toyota) began penetrating the subcompact market that had been successfully opened by Volkswagen, while German cars continued to enjoy popularity. From 1964 to the time of the Arab oil embargo in 1973, the total non-Canadian import share of the domestic market grew from about 6.5 percent to 13.5 percent. Japanese producers' share increased from 0.2 to 8.5 percent, while German producers' share increased from 4.4 to 5.8 percent.

The oil embargo was a major watershed for the U.S. automobile industry. In 1973, domestic purchases of passenger cars peaked at 11.6 and production at 9.7 million vehicles. As the economy recovered from the 1974-75 recession, the U.S. industry enjoyed increased sales through 1978 but, as the economy continued to grow through 1979, automobile sales declined and fell even further with the recession in 1980. In 1979 and 1980, domestic producers bore the burden of declining sales as imports continued to grow. The Japanese import market share grew from 8.5 percent in 1973-75 to 13.6 percent in 1978 and to 15.2 and 22.4 percent in 1979 and 1980, respectively. From 1978 to 1980, U.S. producers' sales declined about 31 percent, from 9.2 million to 6.3 million vehicles, while Japanese sales in the United States increased about 27 percent, from 1.6 to 2.0 million vehicles.

The collapse of U.S. automobile sales after 1978 imposed enormous hardships on the workers and communities dependent on the automobile, tire and steel industries. This decline in sales and the disproportionate burden borne by the U.S. industry and its employees had several sources. Overall, the demand for automobiles was depressed by:

- the dramatic increases in gasoline prices that followed the Iranian revolution—according to the Department of Energy, average city retail gasoline prices increased from about $0.65 per gallon in 1978 to about $0.88 and $1.22 in 1979 and 1980, respectively;

- the slow growth in real disposable income that accompanied the economic slowdown in 1980—historically, automobile sales have been highly cyclical and closely related to consumer disposable incomes and sentiments about the outlook for the economy;

- the substantially higher interest rates that followed the Federal Reserve Board's historic policy shift in October 1979 significantly increased the cost of financing new automobiles.

At the same time, several factors encouraged a shift in demand toward imported (especially Japanese) automobiles.

- Gasoline prices in excess of $1.00 per gallon, coupled with the rising cost of purchasing and financing automobiles, encouraged a shift in consumer preferences toward less expensive subcompact and compact cars.

- Japanese producers were better positioned to compete head on with U.S. producers in the subcompact and compact categories than in the larger vehicles categories because of the greater number and variety of models they offered in these categories and the perception among U.S. consumers about the quality of Japanese subcompact and compact cars.

- Further, the European Community's high tariff on automobiles and NTBs (including quantitative restrictions of various kinds in France, the United Kingdom and Italy) made the United States one of the few, and certainly the largest, unrestricted market for Japanese cars.

In response to the devastating consequences the slump in sales imposed on U.S. workers and automobile-dependent communities, the United Automobile Workers petitioned the International Trade Commission for import relief under the safeguard clause in June 1980. However, in December 1980, the ITC determined that although the domestic automobile industry was hurt by increased imports, imports were not the substantial cause of injury. In a split decision, the commission found other factors, such as the decline in overall demand and the shift toward smaller cars, to be more important causes of the industry's difficulties.

In January 1981, Neil Goldschmidt, the Carter Administration's outgoing Secretary of Transportation, recommended that the United States negotiate temporary restraints on imports with Japan as part of a comprehensive strategy to restructure the automobile industry, which emphasized industry, labor and government cooperation.

By spring 1981, the automotive industry's plight had attracted intense congressional attention, and a bill was introduced to legislate import quotas. In the face of this, the Japanese preferred to negotiate directly with the Reagan Administration. The

Japanese government agreed to restrain exports to the United States for three years, commencing April 1981. During the first year, shipments were to be held to 1.83 million automobiles,* about 9 percent less than the previous 12 months.

During the first year of the agreement (April 1981–March 1982), U.S. car sales continued to decline. New car sales (foreign and domestic) fell 8.3 percent from the previous 12 months, and imports declined 8.9 percent:

U.S. Passenger Car Retail Sales and Imports[18]
(Thousands)

	Retail Sales	Imports Total	Non-Canadian	Japan
April 1980–March 1981	8,842	3,111	2,558	2,012
April 1981–March 1982	8,104	2,834	2,224	1,832

Owing to the depressed state of the automobile market during the first year of the agreement, the decline in total car sales from the previous 12 months (738 thousand vehicles) and total import sales (277 thousand vehicles) far exceeded the decline in Japanese imports imposed by the agreement (180 thousand). Under these circumstances, to estimate the tariff equivalent of the agreement it seems reasonable to assume that during its first year, the agreement reduced Japanese imports by no more than about 180 thousand vehicles. Under this assumption, the agreement offered the automobile industry protection equivalent to a 2.5 percent tariff on all (Canadian and non-Canadian) imports.[19] This is over and above the 1.6 percent average tariff collected on these imports. The equivalent tariff that would have to be applied to non-Canadian imports only to achieve the same effect was estimated to be 3.3 percent. This would be in addition to the 4.2 percent average tariff collected on these imports.

(6) Nondramatic Literary Publications

The Manufacturing Clause of the U.S. Copyright Law requires that nondramatic literary material written in English by an American author, residing in the United States, must be printed in the United States or Canada to obtain full and unqualified copyright protection. Foreign publishers are denied such protection unless certain production processes, including typesetting of raised surface type, platemaking, printing, and binding, are carried out by U.S. printers. This clause has been in effect in varying forms since 1891 and was most recently renewed in 1982.

The clause covers the following types of products: books, catalogs, directories, periodicals, newspapers, copyrighted commercial printing and business forms, greeting cards, copyrighted advertising material, and other copyrighted materials.

The book printing industry and its workers would be most directly affected by repeal of the Manufacturing Clause. During the debate over renewal of the clause,

---

*This includes 1.68 million cars exported to the United States plus 70,000 cars shipped to Puerto Rico and 82,500 Japanese "vans" (mostly four-wheel drive cars).

they expressed concern that its repeal would result in a substantial loss of employment to Far East producers (e.g., Japan, Hong Kong, Singapore, Indonesia, South Korea, Taiwan, and possibly China). The Congressional Research Service surveyed and evaluated various estimates of the potential effects on import penetration of repealing the Manufacturing Clause and made estimates of its own employing an econometric model.[20] On the basis of its own estimates and those computed by others, the Congressional Research Service estimated import penetration could rise to 10–19 percent after long-run adjustments if the Manufacturing Clause were repealed.[21] The estimated tariffs that could have the equivalent impact on imports would be 31.2 to 42.4 percent.[22] This industry receives no tariff protection.

SAFEGUARD (ESCAPE CLAUSE) ACTIONS

As briefly discussed earlier, GATT signators may temporarily increase protection to industries experiencing sudden or serious injury from import surges by resorting to Article XIX, the main safeguard provision in the GATT. Before taking emergency action, a country must demonstrate that increased imports of a given product are causing, or threatening to cause, serious harm to domestic producers of similar or directly competitive products.

Figure 2–1 summarizes the safeguard actions taken by various governments from 1971 to 1981. Given the amount of trade liberalization that has been achieved over the last 30 years, the number and breadth of actions taken by AICs has been limited. But Article XIX has been frequently bypassed by AICs. As described in the preceding section, the United States has worked through official channels on a bilateral basis to negotiate OMAs that limit imports in trade-impacted sectors. The European Community also has limited imports from Japan and the NICs through agreements achieved both through bilateral negotiations and through unofficial industry-to-industry agreements. The threat of legislative and administrative action has been used to leverage the acceptance of restrictions on exports to Europe. Affected imports in Europe have included many of the same products that have been the focus of U.S. trade restrictions—for example, color televisions, footwear and automobiles.

Under U.S. law (the Trade Act of 1974), an industry qualifies for safeguard action if increased imports are a *substantial*[23] cause of injury or threat of injury. The affected industry (firms or unions) requests an investigation by the ITC, and a determination is made as to whether injury from increased imports is occurring. If an affirmative decision is reached, the ITC recommends a remedy to the President, who must impose or modify this remedy within 60 days. The ultimate remedy may be higher tariffs, tariff quotas, other types of direct quantitative limits on imports, OMAs, or adjustment assistance. If the President's decision on injury or remedy varies from the ITC's recommendation, Congress has 90 legislative days to override the President by a simple majority vote and enforce the ITC's recommendation.

Since 1975, the United States has imposed safeguard measures on six products.[24] Additional tariffs were levied on selected product categories, and quotas were placed on clothespins.

More detailed information is provided in Table 2–7, including sources of supply and the value of imports affected. The products involved tend to be less skilled-labor intense in production or capital intense and standardized, and often Japan or an industrializing less developed country is the principal supplier.

FIGURE 2-1. SAFEGUARD ACTIONS TAKEN BY VARIOUS GOVERNMENTS, 1971-81[1]

Country	Product	Measure[2]	Year Introduced
Australia	Footwear	QR	1974
	Motor vehicles	QR	1975
	Certain apparel items	T	1975
	Sheets and plates of iron and steel	QR	1975
	Ophthalmic frames, sunglasses	QR	1975
	Files and rasps	QR	1976
	Knitted and woven dresses	T	1976
	Electric freezer chests	QR	1976
	Passenger motor vehicles	QR	1977
	Brandy	T and TQ	1977
	Fired resistors	QR	1977
	Wool worsted yarns	TQ	1978
	Double-edged safety razor blades	QR	1978
	Sheets and plates of iron and steel	QR	1978
	Certain work trucks and stackers	QR	1980
Canada	Strawberries	T	1971
	Men's and boys' shirts, woven or knitted	QR	1971
	Fresh cherries	T	1973
	Live cattle and beef	T	1973
	Cattle, beef and veal	QR	1974
	Worsted spun acrylic yarns	QR	1976
	Work gloves	QR	1976
	Certain textured polyester yarns	T	1976
	Fresh and frozen beef and veal	QR	1976
	Double-knit fabrics	QR	1976
	A range of clothing items	QR	1976
	Certain footwear	QR	1977
EC	Tomato concentrates	QR	1971
	Timber (Germany only)	QR	1973
	Magnetophones (Italy only)	QR	1973
	Bovine meat and live cattle	QR/E	1974
	Peaches	E	1974
	Preserved mushrooms	QR	1974
	Frozen hake fillets (France only)	E	1975
	Tunny (France only)	E	1975
	Portable TV sets from S. Korea	QR	1977
	Squid (Italy only)	QR	1977
	Preserved cultivated mushrooms	QR	1978
	Yarn of synthetic fibers (UK only)	QR	1980
Finland	Women's pantyhose	T	1976
Iceland	Furniture, cupboards, cabinets, windows, and doors	D	1979
Israel	Radio equipment	T	1971
Japan	Bovine meat	QR	1974
New Zealand	Fabrics	QR	1975
Norway	Various textile items	QR	1978
Spain	Selected heterocyclic compounds; nucleic acids	T	1979
	Cheeses	NA	1980
Switzerland	Bottled white wines	QR	1975
	Bottled red wines	TQ	1976

(Continued on p. 30)

FIGURE 2-1. Continued

Country	Product	Measure[2]	Year Introduced
United States	Ceramic tableware	T	1972
	Ball bearings	T	1974
	Certain dried milk	E	1976
	Stainless and alloy tool steel	QR (OMA)	1976
	Footwear	BRA	1977
	CB radio receivers	T	1978
	High carbon ferrochromium	T	1978
	Lag screws or bolts	T	1979
	Clothespins	QR	1979
	Porcelain-on-steel cookware	T	1980
	Mushrooms	T	1981

1 Not all the notifications to the GATT listed here specifically mention Article XIX.
2 Letters indicate the following: BRA = bilateral restraint agreement; E = embargo; OMA = orderly marketing agreement; QR = quantitative restriction; T = tariff; TQ = tariff quota; D = import deposits; NA = not available.

Product	Dates	Standing Tariff	Additional Protection
Porcelain-on-steel cookware	1980–84	3.3%	8.8–17.6%
Clothespins	1979–85	16.8	28.2
Industrial fasteners	1979–82	4.0	10.9
High carbon ferrochromium	1978–82	0.6	n.a.
CB radios	1978–81	6.0	9–15
Ceramic tableware	1976–78	21.4–23.1	21.5–22.5

CUSTOMS VALUATION

Customs valuation is the process by which customs officials assign imports a tariff classification and a unit value. Based on these determinations, an import duty is then assessed according to one of three types of rates: a specific rate (an amount per unit), an *ad valorem* rate (on a percentage of the unit value), or a compound rate (on a combination of specific and *ad valorem* rates). Thus, the amount of the duty assessed an import is highly contingent on the systems used to assign goods to tariff classifications and to assign values to goods.

Customs valuation procedures may become NTBs if customs officials arbitrarily assign goods to classifications with higher tariff rates than the goods would normally pay or assign goods higher values than are appropriate. Further, they may become NTBs if customs procedures create uncertainty for importers as to the tariff classification or the value that will be assigned products.

U.S. tariff rates are generally applied to the price of the import in the exporting country—that is, the f.o.b. value. However, prior to the implementation of the Customs Valuation Code negotiated in the Tokyo Round, some goods were purposely assigned

TABLE 2-7. U.S. SAFEGUARD ACTIONS IN PLACE AND THEIR ESTIMATED TARIFF EQUIVALENTS, 1975-81

Product (TSUS Nos.[1] and SIC Codes)	Affected Countries	Effective Dates	Action	Standing Tariff (ad valorem[2])		Additional Protection (Percent)		Assumed Elasticity[3]	Imports ($ Millions)	
Porcelain-on-steel cookware TSUS: 653.97 (changed to 654.0207) SIC: pt 3469	Major: Mexico, Taiwan, S. Korea	1/17/80–1/16/84	Additional tariffs on all U.S. imports of porcelain-on-steel cookware valued at or below $2.25 per pound, except tea kettles. Additional tariffs are 20, 20, 15, and 10 cents per pound, respectively, in the 1st, 2nd, 3rd, and 4th years of protection.	1979	3.3%	1980 1981 1982 1983	17.6[4] 17.6 13.2 8.8	n.a.	1978:	$33
Clothespins TSUS: 790.05 SIC: pt 2499 pt 3079	Major: PRC, Taiwan Others include: Poland, W. Germany, Rumania, the Netherlands	2/79–2/85	Global quota for three years in amount of two million gross yearly valued at no more than $1.70 gross. Quota to be administered quarterly, with value breakdown as follows: Category — Yearly Quota Valued not over $.50 per gross — 500,000 gross Valued between $.80–1.35 per gross — 600,000 gross Valued between $1.36–1.70 per gross — 900,000 gross	1978	16.8	1979–81	28.2[5]	1.44	1978	3[6]
Bolts, nuts, large screws (industrial fasteners) TSUS: 646.49, 54, 56, 63 SIC: pt 3452	Major: Japan Others include: Taiwan, India, EC, Spain	1/6/79–1/5/82	Tariffs increased for three years to 15 percent for large screws, including lag screws (TSUS 646.49); and to 15 percent plus previous specific rates of duty for bolts and nuts.	1978 (overall)	4.0	1979–81 (overall)	10.9	n.a.	1978 1979	333.8 378.6
High carbon ferrochromium TSUS: 607.31 SIC: pt 3313	Major: S. Africa Others include: Yugoslavia, Sweden, sometimes Brazil	11/78–11/82	Tariffs increased for three years by $.04 per pound on imports valued at less than $.38 per pound. Once prices rise to equal $.38 per pound, no additional duty will be charged.	1978	0.6	Cannot be estimated		n.a.	1978 1979	78.3 94.8
CB radios TSUS: 685.25 (changed to 685.28 and then to 685.27) SIC: pt 3662	Major: Japan Others include: Taiwan, S. Korea, Hong Kong	4/11/78–4/10/81	Tariffs increased from 6 percent to 21 percent in the first year, 18 percent in the second year, and 15 percent in the third year. Rate then returns to 6 percent.	1977	6.0	1978 1979 1980	15.0 12.0 9.0	n.a.	1977 1978 1979	454.6 163.0 56.8
Ceramic tableware TSUS: 533.28, 38, 73, 75 (changed to 923.01, 07, 13, 15) SIC: pt 3262 pt 3263	Major: Japan, U.K.	5/1/76–10/6/78 (1972 action extended in 1976 for certain categories)	Tariff increases granted in 1972 were continued for four TSUS categories at the then prevailing rates for one year. These increases were scheduled to decline over the next two years and to terminate on 4/30/79. All protection was terminated on 10/6/78. The TSUS categories and their rates are as follows: 5/1/76–4/30/77 533.28 10¢/DZP + 21% ad val. 533.38 10¢/DZP + 21% ad val. 533.73 10¢/DZP + 48% ad val. 533.75 10¢/DZP + 55% ad val. 5/1/77–4/30/78 533.28 8.5¢/DZP + 17.5% ad val. 533.38 8.5¢/DZP + 17.5% ad val. 533.73 8.5¢/DZP + 39.5% ad val. 533.75 8.5¢/DZP + 47% ad val. 5/1/78–10/5/78 533.28 7¢/DZP + 14% ad val. 533.38 7¢/DZP + 14% ad val. 533.73 7¢/DZP + 31% ad val. 533.75 7¢/DZP + 38.5% ad val.	1976 1977 1978	22.6 23.1 21.4	1976 1977 1978	21.5 22.5 22.4	n.a.	1976 1977 1978 (first 10 months)	3.2 2.4 1.9

1 In some instances, the TSUS number for products protected under the escape clause includes other products not granted special protection. In these cases, a new TSUS category is set up to allow Customs and other interested parties to segregate the amount of the restrained goods being imported, their value and the duties collected.
2 Unless otherwise specified, this is the average ad valorem tariff in the absence of supplemental protection.
3 Assumed import elasticity is reported when employed to estimate the tariff equivalent. In these cases, the percentage change in imports induced by the quantitative restriction was divided by the elasticity to obtain the estimated tariff equivalent.
4 Estimates based on 1978 import data.
5 Estimates based on 1976–78 production, consumption, imports, and prices.
6 This value is estimated from data for the first six months of 1978.
Estimation: The additional protection afforded porcelain-on-steel cookware, industrial fasteners and ceramic tableware was obtained by computing the additional duty collected and then dividing by the value of affected imports. For clothespins, the anticipated import share was compared to 1976–77 to estimate a 37.2 percent reduction in imports. The formula in footnote 8 in the text was then applied to obtain the estimated additional protection. For CB radios, ad valorem tariffs were raised; therefore, an estimation was not required.

Sources: Column 1: ITC Publication Nos. 852, 893, 911, 921, 933, and 1008; ITC; and authors' estimates.
Column 2: ITC Publication Nos. 852, 893, 911, 933, and 1008; U.S. Trade Representative press release, December 26, 1978.
Column 3: General Agreement on Tariffs and Trade, L/3700/Add. 2. May 14, 1976; L/4634/Add. 2, May 3, 1978; L/4702/Add. 1, December 6, 1978; L/4742/Add. 1, January 30, 1979; L/4759/Add. 1, March 12, 1979; L/4889/Add. 1, January 22, 1980 (Geneva, Switzerland).
Column 4: Trade Action Monitoring System, Office of the U.S. Trade Representative (Washington), various issues; Trade Representative press release, February 8, 1979; and ITC.
Column 5: U.S. Trade Representative press releases, January 2, 1980 (and undated); IM 146, Department of Commerce (1976, 1977, 1979); and authors' estimates.
Column 6: Trade Action Monitoring System, Office of the U.S. Trade Representative (Washington), October 10, 1980; IM 146, Department of Commerce (1979); and authors' estimates.
Column 7: Authors' estimates.
Column 8: U.S. Trade Representative press release, January 2, 1980; IM 146, Department of Commerce (1977, 1978, 1979); and ITC.

higher values under Final List and American Selling Price (ASP) provisions of U.S. customs valuation procedures.

(1) U.S. Valuation System Prior to 1980

Before the changes brought about by the Tokyo Round, U.S. customs officials worked with nine possible valuation standards to appraise imports. Five of these criteria were established by *Section 402a* of the *Tariff Act of 1930*. These were later replaced for most goods by four new criteria in *Section 402* by the *Customs Simplification Act of 1956*. Although the names of the methods in the two sections were the same or similar, technical differences in definition resulted in different valuations.

In response to objections by import-competing domestic producers that the new Section 402 standards yielded lower valuations for some products, the Treasury Department established a Final List of 1,015 products (on which the dutiable values for fiscal year 1954 would have been reduced by 5 percent or more if appraised under the 402 standards) to be valued according to the old 402a rules. All imports *not* on this Final List were valued according to the newer 402 standards.

In addition, customs regulations required that imports on a selected list be valued at ASP regardless of the potential applicability of other standards. Under Section 402a and Section 402 criteria, U.S. customs officials valued products at their cost to importers in the foreign country—i.e., net of transportation costs to the United States—unless ASP valuation was required. Under ASP, goods were valued at the wholesale price of the U.S. counterpart.[25] ASP valuation tended to impose customs values higher than the goods cost importers in the exporting country because U.S. wholesale prices tend to be higher than foreign port prices for U.S. import-competing products. Thus, ASP provided U.S. producers of import-competing goods with an extra measure of protection.

The bulk of 1977 imports, 82 percent, were valued under 402 standards, while 14 percent of U.S. imports were subject to 402a Final List valuation. Within these groups, ASP valuation accounted for less than 1 percent of 1977 imports (see Table 2–8).

(2) Post-Tokyo Round Customs Valuation Procedures

Complaints that customs valuation procedures, regulations and practices constitute NTBs stem from views that:

- customs valuation procedures may permit or compel officials to arbitrarily assign high values to imports;

- the tariff nomenclature is unnecessarily complex and difficult to interpret, allowing officials to assign imports arbitrarily to high duty classifications;

- the complexity of the tariff nomenclature and customs valuation procedures is such that importers are uncertain as to what rates of duty and values will be applied before making commitments to purchase and ship products;[26] and

- the complexity of customs valuation procedures makes the process of documenting imports unnecessarily time-consuming and expensive.

Prior to the Tokyo Round, Final List, ASP and documentation requirements (specifically Special Customs Form 5515) were frequently cited by U.S. trading partners as NTBs. The Final List was originally designed as a temporary means by which certain industries could gain time to "adjust" to the new, lower valuation of competitive imports. But exporters to the United States asserted that the time had long since run out for this vaguely defined, tedious list and that its continued maintenance constituted a nontariff barrier. Similarly, the ASP became, to some U.S. trading partners, a symbol of U.S. protectionism, particularly of the chemical industry. It was charged that the ASP permitted domestic manufacturers to manipulate the level of tariff protection against imports by adjusting the price for domestic products[27] and that very often an importer did not know whether the import would be subject to ASP until the duty had been assessed.[28]

The Customs Valuation Code that emerged from the Tokyo Round went into effect in the United States on July 1, 1980 and sets out a five-tiered valuation system effectively eliminating ASP and Final List from the U.S. customs valuation process. The value of an import is now determined primarily on the basis of the good's transaction value (for U.S. imports, the f.o.b. price *actually* paid).

(3) Impact of the Customs Valuation Code on U.S. Valuation Procedures

This new Customs Valuation Code is basically very similar to the U.S. system under Section 402. The only real change in the new code for the United States is the elimination of Final List and ASP. A 1979 ITC study concluded that, since less than 5 percent of U.S. imports in 1977 were appraised on the basis of ASP or Final List, "on an overall basis the probable economic effect of U.S. adoption of the ... code would be minimal."[29] In particular, the ITC determined that the new system would only adversely impact the benzenoid chemical, rubber footwear and canned clam industries by eliminating ASP, and the ball and roller bearing and certain tire industries by eliminating the Final List.[30]

In formulating U.S. tariff offers in the Tokyo Round, the United States prepared a schedule of upward-adjusted or converted tariff rates that compensated for the duties lost by eliminating ASP and Final List. These higher tariff rates provided the point of departure for U.S. tariff-cut offers in these categories.

TABLE 2-8. DISTRIBUTION OF CUSTOMS ENTRIES BY BASES OF VALUATION, 1977

Section 402a (Final List)	Percent 1977 Imports	Section 402	Percent 1977 Imports
Foreign value	3.2	—	—
Export value	4.7	Export value	69.5
U.S. value	0.3	U.S. value	1.7
Cost of production	5.5	Constructed value	10.3
ASP	0.6	ASP	0.9
Total 402a*	14.2	Total 402*	82.4

* 402a and 402 totals do not add to 100 percent due to an additional 3.4 percent valued under Section 500, which sets out appraisement, classification and liquidation procedures. This table was compiled from a special survey of all customs import specialist teams by the ITC.
Sources: U.S. Congress, Senate Committee on Finance, Subcommittee on International Trade, *MTN Studies: Part 2, No. 6, Agreements Being Negotiated at the Multilateral Trade Negotiations in Geneva—U.S. International Trade Commission Investigation No. 332-101, Analysis of Nontariff Agreements*, by the International Trade Commission, CP 96-27 (Washington, August 1979), p. D-2.

The analysis that follows bears out that, while ASP and Final List may have provided a significant amount of protection to the producers of some specific products, the overall impact on the broader industries producing these products was small.

American Selling Price

ASP was originally established by the Tariff Act of 1922 to protect the infant benzenoid chemical industry. ASP appraisement was expanded to cover rubber footwear in 1933, canned clams in 1934 and wool knit gloves and mittens not valued over $1.75 per dozen pairs in 1936. No other products were added after 1936.

Table 2-9 presents measures of the protection provided by ASP valuation on 1976 imports of benzenoid chemicals, rubber footwear, canned clams, and wool knit gloves. The second column shows the actual customs value under ASP, while the third column shows the f.a.s. value that closely approximates the f.o.b. value on which *ad valorem* duties would have been applied in the absence of ASP. The fourth column shows the average *ad valorem* duty applied to that product. The additional protection (final column) from ASP may be estimated by multiplying the tariff rate by the difference between the customs and f.a.s. value and dividing by the f.a.s. value.[31]

Where ASP applied, it gave significant additional protection to benzenoid chemical, rubber and plastic footwear and canned clam producers. But the values of imports covered were not large in comparison to the major manufacturing sectors producing these products.

Major Manufacturing Sector (SIC)	Total 1976 Imports ($ Millions)	Percent Covered by ASP	Average Protection Afforded Major Manufacturing Sector (Percent)
Chemicals (28)	3918.9	18.2	0.5
Rubber and plastic products (30)	2032.7	9.4	0.4
Food and kindred products (20)	7098.2	0.1	less than 0.05

Final List

In 1976, Final List articles accounted for about 14 percent of the value of U.S. imports. Table 2-10 presents estimates of the additional protection provided the major manufacturing sectors by Final List. Like ASP, across these broad major industry groups, Final List did not account for large amounts of protection. But for selected products, additional protection from Final List was significant. Of Final List items with imports over $25 million in 1976,[32] tariff rates were raised at least 1 percent for nine items that are listed in Table 2-11.

In 1976, certain pneumatic tires and tubes and ball and roller bearings received the most additional protection. In a study prepared for U.S. Tokyo Round negotiators, the ITC determined that only for these products did the additional protection received

TABLE 2-9. PROTECTION PROVIDED BY ASP VALUATION, 1976
($ Thousands and Percent)

	ASP Customs Value	f.a.s. Value	Average Tariff	Additional Protection
Benzenoid chemicals	$848,078	$710,641	14%	2.7%
Rubber and plastic footwear	234,019	191,876	20	4.3
Canned clams	6,542	5,384	14	3.0
Wool knit gloves	0	0	—	—

Sources: Department of Commerce, *U.S. Imports for Consumption and General Imports*, FT-246 (annual), 1976; and Commerce, IM-146 (monthly), December 1976.

from the Final List have "significant economic effects" for U.S. producers.[33] Therefore, these two products received special attention in formulating U.S. tariff offers.

(4) Tariff Nomenclatures

The Customs Valuation Code does not address the problems of complex, incompatible tariff nomenclatures among trading partners. Rather, over the past 10 years,

TABLE 2-10. ADDITIONAL PROTECTION PROVIDED BY FINAL LIST BY MAJOR SIC SECTOR, 1976

Major Manufacturing Sector (SIC)	Total 1976 Imports ($ Millions)	Percent of Imports Covered by Final List	Average Protection Afforded Entire Industry
Food and kindred products (20)	$7,098.2	3.53	0.002%
Tobacco manufactures (21)	316.4	0	0
Textile mill products (22)	2,023.6	9.18	0.012
Apparel and other textile products (23)	3,288.1	0	0
Lumber and wood products (24)	2,346.3	1.83	*[a]
Furniture and fixtures (25)	515.1	0	0
Paper and allied products (26)	3,276.0	0	0[a]
Printing and publishing (27)	343.2	42.80	0[a]
Chemicals and allied products (28)	3,918.9	6.99	0.009
Petroleum and coal products (29)	6,569.0	0	0
Rubber and miscellaneous plastic products (30)	2,032.7	49.07	0.202
Leather and leather products (31)	1,719.6	0	0
Stone, clay and glass products (32)	1,092.1	4.05	0.014
Primary metal products (33)	8,754.1	0.46	0[a]
Fabricated metal products (34)	1,838.6	1.86	*[a]
Machinery (exc. electrical) (35)	6,670.1	4.50	*[a]
Electric and electronic equipment (36)	8,405.6	19.73	*[a]
Transportation equipment (37)	16,067.7	39.48	0[a]
Instruments and related products (38)	2,251.3	18.94	0.037[a]
Miscellaneous manufactured products (39)	2,559.6	32.43	0.138[a]
Total manufacturing (20-39)	81,086.2	14.28	0.001

* = Less than 0.0005 percent.
a Part of this sector is included in Miscellaneous manufactured products (39); therefore, the average rate of protection is biased upward for SIC 39 and biased downward for this sector.
Source: Derived from data in U.S. Congress, Senate Committee on Finance, Subcommittee on International Trade, *MTN Studies: Part 2, No. 6, Agreements Being Negotiated at the Multilateral Trade Negotiations in Geneva—U.S. International Trade Commission Investigation No. 332-101, Analysis of Nontariff Agreements*, by the International Trade Commission, CP 96-27 (Washington, August 1979), p. D-13.

TABLE 2-11. PRODUCTS WITH 1976 IMPORTS OVER $25 MILLION WHOSE DUTIES WERE RAISED AT LEAST 1 PERCENT BY FINAL LIST

Product	Imports ($ Millions)	Percentage Points Additional Tariffs
Tires and tubes, pneumatic	805.8	6.1
Bearings, roller, metal and parts	68.4	4.5
Sensitized photographic paper	75.5	3.9
Motion picture film	85.5	3.5
Bearings, ball, metal and parts	105.7	3.3
X-ray film	47.4	3.3
Biscuits, cakes, wafers, etc.	50.0	2.2
Synthetic rubber	76.3	2.2
Cameras	174.1	1.7

Source: U.S. Congress, Senate Committee on Finance, Subcommittee on International Trade, *MTN Studies: Part 2, No. 6, Agreements Being Negotiated at the Multilateral Trade Negotiations in Geneva—U.S. International Trade Commission Investigation No. 332-101, Analysis of Nontariff Agreements*, by the International Trade Commission, CP 96-27 (Washington, August 1979), pp. D-14-16.

discussions have been under way between the United States and other concerned countries in the Customs Cooperation Council in an effort to develop a uniform product classification system.

Using the Customs Cooperation Council Nomenclature as its base (the CCCN is essentially the new name of the Brussels Tariff Nomenclature, used by all major trading countries except Canada and the United States), the council developed a "new" nomenclature, known as the Harmonization System. Although the United States actively participated in the work of the council during the past 10 years, it has not yet adopted the new system and, as congressional approval is required to convert to the new nomenclature, its adoption by the United States is not expected before at least the end of 1983.

Several problems stand in its way. In addition to requiring congressional approval, converting the present U.S. tariff nomenclature to the Harmonization System would combine some items, thereby changing tariffs and potentially breaking some of the tariff bindings of the Tokyo Round negotiations.

(5) Costs Imposed by U.S. Customs Documentation Requirements

Customs documentation requirements become NTBs when compliance is excessively complex, formal, costly, lengthy, and time consuming. A 1971 Department of Transportation (DOT) study found that one year's trade with the United States consisting of 10 million export shipments and 8 million import shipments generated 828 million documents and more than 1 billion manhours of work.[34]

U.S. Special Customs Invoice 5515 has been the object of strong criticism from exporters to the United States for some time. The exporter is required to fill out this invoice for every shipment of goods to the United States valued in excess of $500. Critics maintain that the form is too complex, detailed, virtually impossible to complete accurately, and requires information beyond that normally required by most countries for valuation or statistical purposes.[35] The 1971 DOT study calculated the average cost of preparing Invoice 5515 to be $11.31, and the average manhours needed to prepare it to be 1 hour and 25 minutes.[36] This estimate was updated employing a wage index for clerical workers. In 1976, $128,873 million in imports generated 3.6 million 5155 forms that cost approximately $55.3 million to fill out. In 1979, $205,923 million imports generated 4.4 million forms at an estimated cost of $83.2 million to complete.[37]

EXCISE TAXES

In addition to import tariffs, importers must pay excise and sales taxes that are applicable to comparable domestic products. These taxes become NTBs if they are administered in such a way that imported goods pay higher taxes than their domestic counterparts. Before the Tokyo Round agreements became effective, the U.S. federal excise tax on distilled beverages was in this category.

When distilled spirits were taxed by the *wine-gallon method*, a base rate of $10.50 per gallon was assessed on all spirits of 100 proof or less. Therefore, spirits with less than 100 proof were taxed at the same $10.50 per gallon as spirits with exactly 100 proof. Domestic spirits were taxed at the distillery before they were cut and bottled, so producers generally paid $10.50 per 100 proof gallon on the final bottled product. However, imported spirits often arrived in the United States cut and bottled and ended up being more heavily taxed. Foreign competitors could avoid this problem by shipping in bulk and bottling in the United States. For example, the domestic producer of 86 proof gallon whiskey paid a federal excise tax of $9.03 per bottled gallon, while the foreign shipper of an 86 proof bottled whiskey to the U.S. paid a tax of $10.50.[38] Thus, the foreign producer, taxed on a wine-gallon basis, paid $1.47 per gallon more than the domestic producer.

Similarly, a $0.62 import duty was levied on a wine-gallon basis. Therefore, an 86 proof gallon of whiskey paid $0.09 more import duties than comparable whiskey entering the country uncut.

Table 2-12 indicates that an estimated $121 million in additional excise taxes and duties were collected in 1977 because of the wine-gallon method of assessment. The United States imported $674 million of distilled spirits, and the wine-gallon assessment added 18 percentage points to the tariff protection provided U.S. producers.

At the Tokyo Round, several countries, including Canada and those in the EC, requested that the United States eliminate the wine-gallon method of assessing taxes on certain distilled spirits. In return for concessions on other NTBs, the United States offered to work bilaterally to eliminate selectively the assessment method on the specific spirits and tax imports at $10.50 per proof gallon. Tariffs would be increased (equal to the value of foregone revenue) on specific distilled spirits from those countries that did not provide reciprocal concessions. The United States reached bilateral agreements with all of the countries listed in Table 2-12, except Mexico, Spain, Greece, Poland, and Portugal, whose spirits imports are subject to the upwardly revised tariffs. So, it appears this NTB has been eliminated for over 90 percent of U.S. spirit imports.[39]

GOVERNMENT PROCUREMENT

Governments around the world have consistently discriminated against foreign suppliers in favor of domestic producers in procurement. Sometimes these practices

TABLE 2-12. ESTIMATED ADDITIONAL TAX AND DUTY COLLECTED, 1977
($ Thousands)

Country	Amount
United Kingdom	61,763
Canada	37,941
France	9,033
Italy	4,022
Mexico	651
Spain	560
Greece	354
Ireland	353
Jamaica	188
Denmark	187
W. Germany	157
Netherlands	62
Poland	55
Portugal	33
All others	5,963
Total	121,322

Source: U.S. Congress, Senate Committee on Finance, Subcommittee on International Trade, *MTN Studies: Part 4, No. 6, Agreements Being Negotiated at the Multilateral Trade Negotiations in Geneva—U.S. International Trade Commission Investigation No. 332-101, Analysis of Nontariff Agreements*, by the International Trade Commission, CP 96-27 (Washington, August 1979), p. 245.

are enforced and regulated by legislation, but often time-honored traditions dictate purchasing patterns, effectively protecting domestic producers when the government is doing the purchasing. Further, the consequences of these practices often go beyond their effects on government purchases. State-owned corporations frequently follow their government's lead in discriminating against foreign suppliers. And in the case of some large government contracts, discrimination against foreign firms can adversely affect their sales potential elsewhere by denying them the opportunity to use large government installations as reference sites for future orders and by denying them the opportunity to establish a critical mass of sales in the foreign country.

The GATT Government Procurement Code will restrict this practice in the future. The signatories have specified the entities whose purchases will be open to foreign suppliers on the same basis as domestic producers, and only these specified entities (such as agencies, departments) are bound by the code. (As a result, the code often does not apply to purchases of important U.S. exports such as heavy electrical, telecommunications and transportation equipment.) Further, safeguards have been incorporated to ensure transparency in the procurement process and to help promote equal treatment of foreign suppliers. For federal countries like the United States, this code applies only to specified direct federal purchases and not to purchases made by subnational governments. Federal governments may still require buy-national procurement policies in the use of federal funds distributed to subnational governments.

U.S. procurement may be divided into two groups:
- direct federal purchases;
- state and local purchases that
    - employ some federal money;
    - employ no federal money.

(1) Direct Federal Procurement

Prior to implementing the GATT code, the federal government pursued a buy-national policy explicitly set out in the so-called Buy-American legislation and executive orders. This policy is still followed for direct purchases that are not covered by the GATT code and includes the purchases of some federal agencies.

Buy-American legislation, like buy-national practices in other countries, responds to a strong public sentiment that government tax revenue should be spent in a fashion that most benefits the United States. Over the years, other concerns have encouraged Buy-American legislation and executive orders as well. These have varied from an early desire to foster military self-sufficiency to an effort during the Depression to increase domestic employment and raise the incomes of domestic producers. More recently, the Buy-American concept has been defended on balance-of-payment and balance-of-trade bases.[40]

The first Buy-American Act of 1933 restricted all federal purchases for use in the United States to domestic sources unless: (1) the required materials were unavailable domestically; (2) the purchase was not in the public interest; or (3) the cost was prohibitive. The price differential to be applied in comparing foreign and domestic products was not spelled out, but the Department of Defense (DOD) set a standard of 25 percent of the landed, tariff-inclusive price, and this standard was generally followed by all agencies until 1954. In that year, an executive order lowered the minimum differential to 6 percent; but in 1955, the preference for small business firms and firms in depressed areas was raised to 12 percent. The executive order of 1954 also clarified the definition of an imported good by providing that products should be considered to be of foreign origin if 50 percent or more of the total materials cost of the product originated outside the United States.[41]

In 1960, DOD introduced a 25 percent preference in favor of U.S. producers of goods purchased for use abroad, a category previously exempted from the Buy-American legislation. In 1962, DOD took advantage of the discretion allowed by the "minimum" provision in the 1954 executive order and raised the differential to 50 percent of the landed, tariff-exclusive price. The overseas-use differential was also raised to 50 percent, and in 1963, this was extended to all federal agencies except the Agency for International Development (AID).[42]

The restrictions imposed by the Buy-American Act do not apply to federal money spent by the states unless the legislation providing the funds so specifies.

Further, the restrictions imposed by the Buy-American Act are not applied to many Canadian products purchased by the U.S. armed forces, the National Aeronautics and Space Administration (NASA) or the U.S. Coast Guard. Canadian products on an approved list (most of the goods for military use or involved in mutual U.S.-Canadian programs) are treated as goods of domestic origin, with neither a price differential nor duty calculated when bids are evaluated. Canadian products not on this list are exempted by defense agencies from application of the Buy-American Act, but any duty payable must be included. Furthermore, when calculating whether a product is of U.S. origin, any component manufactured in Canada for products on this approved list must be counted as of U.S. origin.[43] However, Canadian products are not exempt from the effects of other federal buy-national legislation, such as buy-national provisions of annual defense appropriation bills discussed below.

Until the implementation of the GATT code on January 1, 1981, the essential characteristics of the Buy-American program for direct federal purchases did not change.

This brief history of the Buy-American legislation makes the U.S. federal policy seem highly restrictive. However, a 1976 General Accounting Office study indicates that foreign suppliers are excluded from federal procurement more for national security reasons and practical constraints than because of the Buy-American legislation.[44]

The GAO study examined 90 percent of all 1974 direct federal procurement and found that national security restrictions excluded 38.2 percent ($17 billion) of all purchases from foreign competition. Another 37.2 percent of purchases were found unsuitable for foreign competition because of various practical constraints—e.g., procurement was for services, research and development, construction materials (sand, gravel, rock, and so on) and sole-source or emergency purchases. And 5.5 percent of purchases were DOD petroleum purchases.[45] Therefore, the effects of Buy-American legislation were limited to less than 20 percent of federal purchases.[46]

However, it is important to note that within this 20 percent, the Buy-American legislation and executive orders were, and in some cases still are, enhanced by other U.S. buy-national legislation.[47] For example, the GAO study found that in 1974, $3.9 billion (8.8 percent) of federal purchases were for textiles, subsistence items, specialty metals, and shipbuilding services restricted to domestic sources because of provisions in the annual Appropriations Act for the DOD.[48] Further, $400 million, or another 0.9 percent of the total studied, fell into the category of "other specific legislation." This included purchases from sources set aside to aid small businesses or areas of high unemployment, and purchases from Indian tribal governments and educational or other nonprofit organizations.[49] Canadian officials argue that these practices effectively exclude Canadian bidders despite the GATT Procurement Code.

(2) State and Local Government Procurement

Purchases Employing Some Federal Money

State and local governments procuring goods and services with money supplied, all or in part, by the federal government may be required to adhere to buy-national policies. When required, the buy-national standards are specified in the legislation.

Buy-national policies are embodied in the Surface Transportation Act (STA) of 1978 (highway and mass transit aid), the Amtrak Improvement Act of 1978, the Rural Electrification Act of 1936, the Public Works Employment Act of 1977, and the Clean Water Act of 1977.[50]

Many of the programs funded by these laws are construction projects. Therefore, they involve a considerable amount of services and materials that may only be purchased close to the site (e.g., sand, gravel, rock, and concrete). But they do at times involve considerable amounts of other goods that move in trade (such as steel, railway rolling stock, buses). In this regard, the STA is a particular irritant to U.S. trading partners, especially Canada.

The STA provides $51 billion for highways and urban mass transportation. The act requires that projects costing more than $500,000 use only U.S. materials (50 percent U.S. content) unless this would not be in the public interest; it would make the cost of rolling stock unreasonably expensive; U.S.-made materials are unavailable; or preferences to U.S. producers increase project costs by at least 10 percent.[51] Since importable materials usually comprise a small portion of total project costs, the last restriction provides a price advantage to domestic producers of much more than 10 percent.

Purchases Employing No Federal Money

As of 1980, 35 states and the District of Columbia had some buy-national or buy-state legislation on the books or similar regulation or practice in place for at least certain aspects of procurement.[52] The majority of the policies provide price preference to U.S. or home-state suppliers, but others simply require that "other things equal," preference be given to U.S. or home-state producers.

(3) Assessing the Effects of Buy-National Policies

The effects of buy-national policies on imports may be estimated by comparing imported goods' share of government purchases with imported goods' share of private-sector purchases. By assuming that in the absence of buy-national policies, on average across all industries, the government's average propensity to import would be equal to that of the private sector, a hypothetical level of imports may be computed for the government. Further, the tariff may be estimated that would reduce imports as much as the buy-national policies appear to reduce imports—the difference between hypothetical and actual government imports. This tariff provides an indication of the restrictive effects of buy-national policies.

To make this estimate on an industry-by-industry basis, industry-by-industry data are required for government purchases of imported goods and total procurement. Similar data are also required for private-sector producers. Unfortunately, such data on federal purchases of imported goods have not been collected since the early 1960s and have never been collected on state and local purchases. However, aggregate data for federal government imports are available from the 1976 GAO study previously discussed. As described in detail in Appendix D, these data were used to estimate the tariff equivalent effects on imports of Buy-American and other buy-national legislation restricting direct federal purchases. It was estimated that federal Buy-American and similar policies restricted imports by about as much as a 0.4 percent tariff.

As noted earlier, data are generally available for state and local government imports, but some data are available for purchases of steel used in federally assisted state and local highways. For the period from November 1976 to June 1978, GAO estimated that 9.5 percent of $1 billion of steel purchased for these highways was imported.[53] Over this same period, imported steel accounted for about 17.5 percent of U.S. purchases. Applying the methodology used for federal procurement, buy-national policies in federal, state and local highway construction were estimated to add about 0.3 percentage points to the 5.9 percent average protection provided the steel industry by tariffs.[54]

(4) The Effects of the GATT Government Procurement Code

As a signator of the GATT Government Procurement Code, the United States provided a list of 53 agencies, departments and commissions whose purchase of goods (but not services as the code only covers services incidental to the purchase of goods) in excess of 150,000 Special Drawing Rights, worth about $190,000, would be open to foreign bidders. In terms of 1979 procurement levels, the agreement freed up about $12.5 billion in federal purchases.[55] In 1979, total federal purchases of durable and nondurable goods were $30.6 billion. Of these, about $11.6 billion were strategic and $18.9 billion were nonstrategic.[56] Thus, it appears that the Procurement Code will eliminate the discriminatory effects of U.S. Buy-American and other buy-national policies on two-thirds of federal nonstrategic purchases.

PRODUCT STANDARDS

Governments impose mandatory and voluntary product standards[57] for many reasons: to protect public health and safety; to facilitate product comparisons; to increase the range of choice available to consumers by harmonizing products.

Standards will always differ among countries because of differences in consumer preferences and objective environmental conditions. These differences will create natural barriers to trade. And the smaller the country, the more likely that unique product standards will be import barriers because of the difficulties in manufacturing products with unique characteristics for small markets. In some cases, though, product standards are purposely designed to exclude or limit imports. Further, administrative procedures for applying standards may discriminate against imports by imposing long waiting times and excessive inspection costs.

(1) Product Standards as NTBs

Establishing criteria to determine which product standards are natural barriers to trade and which are NTBs is difficult. The debate in this area appears to take two approaches, one objective and one subjective. Some advocate labeling a foreign standard an NTB if:

- it unnecessarily differs from the home country standard that has proven adequate for the purpose at hand—for example, in protecting consumer health and safety;

- certification and approval procedures are cumbersome, time consuming and expensive; or

- marking, labeling and packaging requirements differ from other countries.

Such standards *could* apply equally to domestic and foreign firms, while negatively affecting only foreign firms.

In contrast to this "black-or-white" test, a more subjective approach labels a standard a nontariff barrier if its *intent* is to inhibit international trade by discriminating against imported products. This line of reasoning holds that a requirement is not an NTB if it has no restrictive intent, even though it may have an adverse impact on trade. Occasionally, one is talking about standards that apply to the exporting country only, or to exporters differently than domestic firms.

The choice of definition has important consequences for how one measures the quantitative impact of standards on an economy. Since virtually all standards restrict trade, a simple measure of the difference between the present system and a "free" system is insufficient. If one subscribes to the first approach to defining a standard as an NTB, one must attempt to measure the difference in the effect on trade of the existing standard and a rewritten standard that is *not* unnecessarily different from that of the foreign firm's country, or excessively time consuming or expensive to comply with.

To apply the second approach, it is necessary to be able to determine intent. The list of standards examined under this approach would be shorter than the list under the first approach. Here, one could theoretically measure the restrictive impact on trade by focusing on the differences between the effect of the standard on domestic producers and on foreign producers.

(2) U.S. Product Standards

The following sections list U.S. product standards about which other countries or exporters have complained. Some of these may legitimately be viewed as NTBs by one or both of the criteria discussed above, but most are, in fact, just part of the cost of doing business in the United States. It was not possible to quantify the effects of U.S. standards that pose trade barriers.

Industrial and Product Standards

Industrial and product standards apply to weight, size, container size, safety, and impact on the environment. Several standards have been cited as nontariff barriers by exporters to the United States:

- Department of Transportation standard for high pressure gas cylinders. All cargo tanks and *compressed-gas cylinders* must be tested and inspected, during manufacture, in the United States. This latter requirement, like similar ones for other products, imposes a barrier to imports.

- Coast Guard inspection of safety equipment. *Safety equipment* must be inspected, as it is manufactured, by U.S. Coast Guard officials in the United States.

- Underwriters Laboratories inspection guarantee. The UL inspection guarantee is required by certain states, often to obtain insurance, for *electrical appliances and apparatus, medical equipment* and *gas- and oil-burning equipment*. Foreign producers claim it is harder for them to get the seal because of the extra costs of duplicating tests and paying for U.S. inspectors' travel expenses to perform on-site inspections.

- Standards of professional and industrial associations. Standards promulgated by professional and industrial associations are sometimes incorporated into state and local laws; some require testing in the United States and inspection of the foreign plant by the association. For example, the National Sanitation Foundation and the National Board of Fire Underwriters issue standards and regulations affecting *plumbing, heating* and *firefighting equipment* which foreign manufacturers claim discriminate against their products.

- Federal Housing Administration standard for window glass thickness. Before imports of 18-ounce *window glass* began to compete with domestically produced 19-ounce glass, 19-ounces per square foot was the weight of glass usually used in U.S. housing construction. In response to complaints by domestic manufacturers of 18-ounce import competition, the FHA in 1963 made 19-ounce glass the required thickness for FHA-financed housing. Because FHA standards are frequently incorporated into state and local building codes, foreign-produced 18-ounce glass was effectively excluded from the U.S. market.

- Agricultural marketing orders. Marketing orders issued by USDA regulate the grade, size, quality, and maturity of various *vegetables, nuts* and *fruit* sold in the United States. A particularly interesting example: green and ripe tomatoes sold in the United States must have minimum diameters of 2 9/32 inches and 2 17/32 inches, respectively. This marketing order effectively excludes 30 to 50 percent of Mexico's tomato crop, while it affects only a small share of Florida's crop.

- Firearms regulations. While imported *hand guns* must pass rigorous tests, domestically produced guns are not subject to any tests.

- Automobile safety and environmental and fuel-economy standards. In particular, the fuel economy standards of the Energy Policy and Conservation Act of 1975 differentiate between North American-made and foreign cars in computing corporate average fuel economy.

Labeling and Marketing Requirements

Labeling and marketing requirements are designed to give the consumer necessary information about a product or its use. Several such requirements have been cited by foreign producers as barriers to trade due to the excessive cost, difficulty and time associated with compliance:

- Marks of origin. According to U.S. law, imported products must show the country of origin in English indelibly and permanently, and in a conspicuous place. In addition, the Federal Trade Commission (FTC) requires that certain foods manufactured in the United States of imported ingredients be labeled to identify the origin of the ingredients. Foreign suppliers of some products (e.g., structural steel and electric power cable) complain of the difficulty of complying with U.S. origin marking requirements. A broad spectrum of products is affected: *food products, rubber products, brass and copper tubing, steel shapes and bars, pipe, wire rod and hardwood products, radio parts,* and *valve and pressure gauge parts.*

- Labeling of alcoholic beverages. The Federal Alcohol Administration Act requires that labels for *alcoholic beverages* be approved by the Treasury Department (Alcohol, Tobacco and Firearms Division), with copies submitted to customs for each shipment of alcohol to the United States. Foreign producers complain that this labeling procedure is time consuming.

- The National Sanitation Foundation and the National Board of Fire Underwriters issue standards and regulations affecting *plumbing, heating* and *firefighting equipment* that foreign manufacturers claim discriminate against their products.

- New York state labeling requirements. New York requires that the name and address of the manufacturer be printed on all imports of *food products* and other *packaged* goods; there is no similar requirement for U.S.-produced goods.

- U.S. Fair Packaging and Labeling Act. This act requires that labels identify the product, describe it, give the name and address of the manufacturer, packer or distributors, and show the net weight or quantity. Provisions of the act also dictate requirements for marking, size of type and terminology. Producers exporting to the United States complain that these provisions are more stringent than comparable laws in the home country, requiring them to incur the added expense of printing special labels for the U.S. market.

- U.S. Fiber Products Identification Act. All imported *textile fiber products* must be marked with the names and percentages of fibers, name and country of the manufacturer, and wool content, if any. In addition, textile imports must meet the requirements of the Flammable Fabrics Act.

Health and Sanitary Standards

To protect human, animal or plant life and health, governments formulate health and safety standards governing the sanitary conditions under which a product is produced or marketed, the wholesomeness of food products, or the use of additives and pesticides. While it is generally agreed that health and sanitary standards are important means of protecting the health of the general population, producers sometimes complain that the standards of a country to which it wishes to export are excessively restrictive, require the duplication of tests, or are applied in such a manner as to discriminate against imports. Some of the U.S. health and sanitary standards that exporters have complained about include the following:

- The Wholesome Meat Act of 1967. Before *meat* and *poultry products*, particularly sausage, salami and ham, can be imported into the United States, USDA must certify that the inspection programs of the home country are comparable to U.S. inspection programs. The restrictive effects of this practice are limited because USDA sends inspectors abroad to conduct inspection programs. Foreign producers estimated the inspection requirement reduces sales to the U.S. about 20 percent.[58]

- *Milk* and *cream* may be imported into the United States only if the foreign firm has a permit specifying that it meets certain U.S. sanitary requirements.

- U.S. standards for *chocolate* require a higher proportion of butterfat to nonfat milk than is normally found in whole milk.

- California requires *flour* to be enriched with niacin above and beyond Food and Drug Administration (FDA) requirements. Foreign suppliers thus have three choices: supply the entire U.S. market with enriched flour, incur the added expense of supplying different kinds of flour to two U.S. markets, or withdraw from the California market.

Pharmaceutical and Veterinary Standards

Pharmaceutical and veterinary standards—regulations requiring testing, plant inspection, special documentation, and use of pharmacopoeia—may prove to be disincentives to trade when unreasonable delays and expenses are incurred in processing imports into the United States. Prepared and packaged pharmaceuticals are usually affected more than bulk preparations. Complaints about U.S. standards of this sort center around three requirements:

- compulsory inspection of the exporter's plant by U.S. inspectors;

- repetition of research and additional tests;

- submission of documents by the foreign firm from its home office to the U.S. Bureau of Narcotics and Dangerous Drugs, required by the U.S. Comprehensive Drug Abuse Prevention and Control Act before certain pharmaceuticals can be imported, even if the pharmaceuticals are not controlled in the source country.

(3) The Tokyo Round's "Standards Code"

The Agreement on Technical Barriers to Trade (the "Standards Agreement") negotiated at the Tokyo Round does not formulate specific standards. Rather, it merely encourages signers to avoid the use of standards that cause "unnecessary obstacles to international trade," understood (but not defined specifically) to mean requirements that exceed what is necessary to protect a legitimate public-welfare interest, as determined by the country imposing the standard. Public-welfare interest includes public health and safety, national security or fundamental technological change—e.g., rewiring an entire country to harmonize electric voltage levels.

Signers of the code need only accept other countries' testing methods when the importing country is satisfied that those methods are technically sufficient—as determined by the importers. The agreement does not apply to standards or technical regulations already in force, only to those enacted after the agreement enters into force. Signature of the national government to the code does not obligate political subdivisions, private groups or international and regional organizations connected with the signer to comply. In short, the agreement is general, vague and unenforceable (a signer's best efforts at compliance are sufficient, and dispute settlement procedures have no definite provisions for enforcement). In general, then, the Standards Agreement will not affect existing U.S. standards and technical regulations applied to imports to any significant degree, if at all.

OVERVIEW

For 1976, Table 2-13 presents estimates of the average protection, above that already provided by tariffs, received by U.S. manufacturing from NTBs affecting both producer and consumer prices analyzed in this chapter. Overall, in 1976 these NTBs provided additional protection estimated to be equivalent to about a 1.1 percent tariff on all manufactured imports. This is quite small compared to the protection extended by tariffs, 4.9 percent. Furthermore, the protection provided by many of these practices declined substantially or disappeared as the GATT codes governing the use of NTBs were implemented.

Outlook for 1985

As a result of agreements reached in the Tokyo Round, the protection afforded by U.S. customs valuation procedures has been reduced by about 80 percent, while the protection from federal procurement practices declined by about two-thirds. Similarly, the protection received by the excise tax on distilled spirits will almost completely disappear. By 1982, the combined protective effects of all the U.S. NTBs listed

TABLE 2-13. SUMMARY OF PROTECTION PROVIDED U.S. MANUFACTURES BY NTBs AFFECTING PRODUCER AND CONSUMER PRICES, 1976 (ESTIMATED), 1982 AND 1985 (PROJECTED)
(Percent)

	1976	1982	1985
Nontariff barriers	1.07	0.73	0.53
Quantitative restrictions and safeguards	0.37	0.57[a]	0.37[a]
Customs valuation (ASP, Final List, Form 5515)	0.21	0.04[b]	0.04[b]
Excise taxes (distilled spirits)	0.13	0.00[c]	0.00[c]
Government procurement (federal)	0.36	0.12[d]	0.12[d]
Tariffs (c.i.f.)	4.93	4.76	4.07

a This assumes that the United States will continue to restrict apparel imports and to impose safeguard actions on various commodities contributing only small amounts to U.S. imports. Further, it includes estimates of the OMA on Japanese automobiles reported in Table 2-1—2.5 percent. Motor vehicles' share of 1980 total manufactured imports was 8.1 percent, so the estimated effect on total manufactured imports was estimated to be (0.0253)(0.081) = .0020, or 0.2 percent.
b The Customs Valuation Code eliminated the effects of ASP and Final List in 1981.
c The United States has eliminated the effects of the wine-gallon valuation system on imports.
d As indicated in the text, the Procurement Code should reduce the effects of federal buy-national policies by two-thirds.
Source: Authors' estimates.

in Table 2-13 declined by about 30 percent from pre-Tokyo Round (1976) levels. The magnitude of this decline is limited by the restraints on imports of Japanese automobiles. However, if these restrictions expire in 1984, the combined protection of U.S. manufacturing by the NTBs examined in this chapter will likely decline still further. Assuming the restraints on Japanese automobiles expire by 1985, the estimated protection from NTBs affecting producer and consumer prices will then be about 0.5 percent, or about 50 percent of their 1976 level and only 13 percent of the protection provided by tariffs.

Sectoral Data

Table 2-14 shows estimates of the protection provided major manufacturing sectors by quantitative restrictions, safeguards, customs valuation, and excise taxes in 1976. Together these practices accounted for over two-thirds of the protection received from the practices listed in Table 2-13. (Only government procurement has been omitted.) Only three major manufacturing sectors received substantial protection (greater than 1 percent) from the practices:

Major Manufacturing Sector (SIC)	Tariff Equivalent
Printing and publishing (27)	17.37%
(Book printing and publishing—2731-2)	(36.82)
Apparel and other textile products (23)	8.8
Food and kindred products (20)	1.5
(Distilled beverages—2085)	(18.0)
(Canned clams—pt. 2091)	(3.0)

Several industries within other major manufacturing sectors also received high levels of protection:

Industry (SIC)	Rate of Protection
Ceramic tableware (pt. 3262-3)	21.48%
Specialty steel (pt. 3312)	6.00
Benzenoid chemicals (pt. 2865)	2.71

However, with the implementation of the Tokyo Round agreements, the protection afforded by these practices to these sectors and industries has been reduced to near-zero levels, with the exception of printing and publishing and apparel. These industries continue to receive the estimated protection reported in Table 2-14, as the Manufac-

TABLE 2-14. TARIFF EQUIVALENTS OF NTBs THAT AFFECT PRODUCER AND CONSUMER PRICES BY MAJOR SIC SECTOR, 1976
(Percent)

Major Manufacturing Sector (SIC)	Quantitative Restrictions	Safeguards	Customs Valuation		Form 5515	Excise Taxes (Wine Gallon/ Proof Gallon Tax)[2]	Total
			American Selling Price	Final List			
Food & kindred products (20)	—	—	*	—	0.04	1.47	1.52
Wines, brandy & brandy spirits (pt. 2084)						8.39	(8.39)
Distilled, rectified, & blended liquors (2085)						18.00	(18.00)
Canned clams (pt. 2091)			3.01				(3.01)
Tobacco manufactures (21)	—	—	—	—	0.04	—	0.04
Textile mill products (22)	n.e.	—	0	0.01	0.04	—	0.06
Wool knit gloves, less than $1.75 a dozen pairs (pt. 2259)			0[3]				(0)
Apparel & other textile products (23)	8.80	—	—	—	0.04	—	8.84
Lumber & wood products (24)	—	—	—	*[1]	0.04	—	0.04
Furniture & allied products (25)	—	—	—	—	0.04	—	0.04
Paper & allied products (26)	—	—	—	—[1]	0.04	—	0.04
Printing & publishing (27)	17.33	—	—	0[1]	0.04	—	17.37
Book printing and publishing (2731-2)	(36.82[4])						(36.82)
Chemicals & allied products (28)	—	—	0.49	0.01	0.04	—	0.54
Benzenoid chemicals (pt. 2865)	—	—	2.71	—	—	—	(2.71)
Petroleum & coal products (29)	—	—	—	—	0.04	—	0.04
Rubber & miscellaneous plastic products (30)	—	—	0.41	0.20	0.04	—	0.66
Footwear (primarily rubber) (pt. 3021)			4.39				(4.39)
Leather & leather products (31)	—	—	—	—	0.04	—	0.04
Stone, clay & glass products (32)	—	0.06	—	0.01	0.04	—	0.10
Ceramic tableware (pt. 3262,3)		21.48					(21.48)
Primary metal products (33)	0.15	—	—	0[1]	0.04	—	0.19
Specialty steel (pt. 3312)	6.00						(6.00)
Fabricated metal products (34)	—	—	—	*[1]	0.04	—	0.04
Machinery (exc. electrical) (35)	—	—	—	*[1]	0.04	—	0.04
Electric & electronic equipment (36)	—	—	—	*[1]	0.04	—	0.04
Transportation equipment (37)	—	—	—	0[1]	0.04	—	0.04
Instruments & related products (38)	—	—	—	0.04[1]	0.04	—	0.08
Miscellaneous manufactured products (39)	—	—	—	0.14[1]	0.04	—	0.18
Total manufacturing (20-39)	0.44	*	0.17	*	0.04	0.13	0.78

n.e. = not estimable.
* = less than 0.005 percent.
1 Part of this sector is included in SIC 39; therefore, SIC 39 is biased upward and each of these sectors is biased downward.
2 Estimates are based on 1977 data.
3 Imports of wool knit gloves valued at less than $1.75 a dozen pairs ceased in the late 1930s.
4 This is the average of the high and low estimates reported in Table 2-1.
Source: Authors' estimates.

turing Clause of the U.S. Copyright Law and bilateral agreements negotiated under the Multi-Fiber Arrangement continue to moderate the growth in imports.

Also, since 1976 and as discussed in the first two sections of this chapter, several major industries have received temporary relief through limits on imports agreed to by principal exporting countries—i.e., footwear, color televisions, specialty steel, and automobiles. Only automobiles continue to benefit from limits on imports. Also, six highly specialized product lines listed in Table 2-1 received temporary safeguard protection.

Practices of Other AICs

Detailed empirical information about the kinds of NTBs examined in this chapter imposed by other AICs is not available; yet it is important to note that other AICs have protected many of the same industries receiving protection in the United States. Important examples include automobiles, textiles and apparel, footwear, color televisions, and food products, as well as various high technology products and service areas in which the United States has a comparative advantage. An exhaustive review of these trade actions is beyond the scope of this study; only some illustrations are offered here.

As described above, Canada requires U.S. automobile companies to meet certain production requirements to benefit from the U.S.-Canadian 1965 Automotive Agreement. Further, Canada has followed the United States in obtaining limits on imports from Japan and has negotiated duty remission schemes with European producers to encourage auto parts production there. The United Kingdom, France and Italy have in various ways limited Japanese imports as well. For its part, Japan imposes taxes on automobiles that increase with engine size, thus discriminating against larger North American and German cars, and has a complicated multilayered distribution system that foreign producers have difficulty penetrating.

Canada, Japan and the countries of the European Community have imposed a variety of measures to limit textile and apparel imports through the MFA and other means. For example, in 1979 Canada limited textile and apparel imports through global quotas, and in 1978 the EC limited imports through 29 different actions. Moreover, during the recent negotiations to review the MFA, the EC sought a more stringent agreement. In the MFA renewed in December 1981, wording was included that will permit the EC to reduce imports below existing levels.

Footwear is no exception. At various times Canada, the United Kingdom and Japan have taken formal actions to limit imports. More recently, the British Footwear Manufacturing Federation signed an agreement with the Taiwan Foot Exporters Association limiting their exports to the United Kingdom in 1981.

In 1977, Canada imposed a surtax on color television imports, and the United Kingdom imposed a quota on black and white televisions. In 1981, Japan agreed to limit color television exports to the EC after the EC expressed concern about a trade imbalance.

In food products, Japanese and EC agricultural policies effectively limit U.S. access to their markets for processed food and other agriculture-based manufactured products.

Furthermore, many U.S. trading partners have become involved in TDPs not generally practiced by the United States that may circumvent the GATT codes governing NTBs. Of particular concern to the United States are performance requirements applied to foreign investors that encourage multinational corporations (MNCs) to undertake activities in host countries—e.g., production, local sourcing, R&D, and management activities—that would normally reside in the MNC's home country or elsewhere. These actions often reduce imports and encourage exports. These practices have potentially ominous consequences for employment in the United States, the world's largest source of capital. Major AICs imposing performance requirements directly affecting imports and/or exports include West Germany, France, Italy, and Canada. Major AICs imposing other performance requirements include Japan and the United Kingdom. Major newly industrializing countries that have performance requirements affecting imports and exports include Brazil, Mexico and Singapore.[59]

Notes

1   Practices that restrict imports are normally expected to increase prices faced by consumers. However, in some circumstances, when domestic and imported goods are imperfect substitutes and protection is temporary, domestic industry costs and prices could decline in the long run. A "breathing spell" may permit the domestic industry to invest, modernize and achieve productivity gains that might not be possible because of imperfections in capital markets without import relief.

2   The United States and other AICs impose limits on imports of various selected agricultural products.

3   Safeguard quotas have been imposed on specialty steel (1976-79) and clothespins (1979-82).

4   It is important to note that, from 1975 to 1980, only 9 of the 45 industries seeking safeguard relief received protection, either through OMAs or direct safeguard action. Moreover, in most cases the product coverage was narrow, limiting the effects on trade of the actions taken.

5   International Trade Commission, *Nonrubber Footwear*, ITC Publication No. 1139 (Washington, 1981), p. A-50.

6   ITC, *Economic Effects of Export Restraints*, ITC Publication No. 1256 (Washington, 1982).

7   The selection of appropriate import elasticities for this computation and all other estimates reported in this study are discussed in Appendix C, which reviews methodology.

8   The ITC study cited in footnote 6 reported an import demand elasticity equal to 4.07. Applying this elasticity, a c.i.f. tariff (t) equal to 9.2 percent and an import reduction (ΔM) equal to 7.12 percent, the tariff equivalent (t_e) may be computed as follows:

$$t_e = \frac{\Delta M (1 + t)}{e} = \frac{(.0712)(1.092)}{4.07} = 1.9$$

This formula is discussed in Appendix C.

9   This is obtained by applying the formula in footnote 8 with $e = 2.8$, $t = 5$ percent and $\Delta M = 35.7$ percent.

10 *Report to the President: A Comprehensive Program for the Steel Industry* (Washington, 1977), often referred to as the Solomon Report.

11 Hot-rolled sheet and strip, 6.8 percent; cold-rolled sheet, 5.1 percent; plate, 5.4 percent; structurals, 9.9 percent; wire rods, 4.3 percent; hot-rolled bars, 2.4 percent; coated sheet, 3.3 percent; tin plate, 2.2 percent; rails, 8.9 percent; and sheet piling, 21.9 percent.

12 ITC, *Stainless Steel and Alloy Tool Steel,* ITC Publication No. 968 (Washington, 1979), p. A-141.

13 Agreements with Taiwan and China were negotiated under provisions of Section 204 of the Agriculture Act of 1956. Their terms are similar to those under the MFA despite the fact that these two countries are not signators to the MFA.

14 SIC major industry 22 (textiles) as reported in the Department of Commerce, *U.S. Industrial Outlook* (Washington), various issues.

15 This is obtained by applying the formula in footnote 8 with $e = 3.66$, $t = 23.1$ percent and $\Delta M = 26.2$ percent.

16 Commerce, *Industrial Outlook,* 1981, p. xxiv.

17 Time series export, import and shipments data are available at the four-digit SIC level. At this level of disaggregation, information about export-competitive sectors are often mixed with comparable information about import-competing sectors.

18 Retail sales data are from the Motor Vehicle Manufacturers Association; import data are from the Department of Commerce.

19 This is obtained by applying footnote 8 with $e = 2.4$, $t = 1.6$ percent and $\Delta M = 5.97$ percent.

20 Congressional Research Service, "Economic Concerns Relating to the Elimination of the Manufacturing Clause of the U.S. Copyright Law," Appendix E to the Copyright Office's report on the Manufacturing Clause (Washington, 1981).

21 Ibid., p. 168.

22 This is obtained by applying the formula in footnote 8 with $e = 1.4$, $t = 0$ and $\Delta M = 43.6$ to 59.5 percent.

23 "Important and not less than any other causes"; see William Cline et al., *Trade Negotiations in the Tokyo Round: A Quantitative Assessment* (Washington: Brookings Institution, 1978), p. 203.

24 Other than OMA products discussed in the previous section.

25 Under the old law, export value based valuation on the wholesale f.o.b. price at which the product was offered for sale to U.S. importers. Foreign value relied on the price in the exporting country plus packing costs. The U.S. value deducted all costs and expenses incurred in exporting the good (such as c.i.f. charges and resale profit in the United States) from the U.S. resale price to approximate the value in the exporting country. Just as its name implies, the cost of production appraised an import's value on the basis of the costs and expenses of producing and packing the product for shipment to the United States (f.a.s. value). However, the American Selling Price (defined alike in 402 and 402a) valued *selected* imports on the basis of the wholesale selling price of U.S. goods that were identical or similar to the imported good, regardless of the actual transaction price of the import. According to an ITC survey of 1977 imports, over one-third of Final List imports were valued using the cost of production method, owing primarily to strict requirements and definitions in export value, foreign value and the constructed value (see Table 2-8).

26 Customs officials were required to determine for every import potentially subject to ASP whether a domestically produced product like or similar to the import was being freely offered for sale in the United States. Often there might be several such products available, and the customs official had to make the subjective and time-consuming decision as to which product was most similar to the import.

27 U.S. General Accounting Office, *Changes Needed in U.S. Valuation System for Imported Merchandise*, GGD-79-29 (March 23, 1979), p. 35.

28 American Importers Association, Inc., *United States Non-Tariff Barriers to Trade*, A Statement in connection with U.S. Tariff Commission Investigation #332-66 (March 1972), p. 27.

29 U.S. Congress, Senate Committee on Finance, Subcommittee on International Trade, *MTN Studies: Part 2, No. 6, Agreements Being Negotiated at the Multilateral Trade Negotiations in Geneva—U.S. International Trade Commission Investigation No. 332-101, Analysis of Nontariff Agreements*, by the International Trade Commission, CP 96-27 (Washington, August 1979), p. 54.

30 Ibid., pp. 26-27.

31 Ibid., p. 83.

32 Items with imports over $25 million comprised 90 percent of Final List imports.

33 Congress, *MTN Studies*, p. 84.

34 Department of Transportation, International Trade Documentation and Office of Facilitation, *Paperwork and Profits* (New York: NCITD, 1971).

35 American Importers Association, *U.S. Non-Tariff Barriers*, pp. 27-28.

36 DOT, *Paperwork and Profits*, p. 112.

37 According to the the data for average compensation of clerical employees published in the *Statistical Abstracts of the United States*, 1 hour and 25 minutes of clerical work should have risen to $15.29 in 1976 and to $18.72 in 1979.

38 U.S. Congress, Senate Committee on Finance, Subcommittee on International Trade, *MTN Studies, Part 4, No. 6, Agreements Being Negotiated at the Multilateral Trade Negotiations in Geneva—U.S International Trade Commission Investigation No. 332-101, Analysis of Nontariff Agreements*, by the International Trade Commission, CP 96-27 (Washington, August 1979), p. 238.

39 In Table 2-12, the revenue collected from Mexico, Spain, Greece, Poland, Portugal, and all others comprise only 6.3 percent of total revenue.

40 These sentiments are especially strong at the state and local levels, where there often is much feeling that it is unpatriotic for government not to support those it represents by purchasing from local or at least domestic sources.

41 J. David Richardson, "The Subsidy Aspects of a 'Buy American' Policy in Government Purchasing" (Washington: U.S. Congress, Joint Economic Committee, June 1972), pp. 222-223.

42 Ibid., p. 223.

43 OECD, *Government Purchasing* (Paris, 1976), p. 128.

44 GAO, *Governmental Buy-National Practices of the United States and Other Countries* (Washington, 1976).

45 Ibid., p. 32. Restrictions on DOD purchases shift private purchases to imported sources.

46 Of course, foreign governments could make similar arguments with respect to composition of their purchases. Further, if some purchases excluded from foreign competition for national security reasons need not be so excluded, these data would then understate the potential protective effects of buy-national legislation.

47 The term Buy-American is used here to refer to the Buy-American Act and executive orders pertaining to its implementation. The term buy-national is broader and refers to all federal and state laws requiring preferences to domestic producers.

48 The exemption of Canadian goods from the application of the Buy-American law in defense purchases does not extend to other buy-national legislation.

49 GAO, *Governmental Buy-National Practices,* pp. 16-17.

50 GAO, *Foreign-Source Procurement Funded Through Programs by State and Local Organizations* (Washington, 1978).

51 Ibid., pp. 17-18.

52 Canadian Department of Industry, Trade and Commerce.

53 GAO, *Foreign-Source Procurement,* p. 27.

54 SIC 3312, 5, 6, and 7.

55 Data was obtained from the Office of the U.S. Trade Representative.

56 These amounts were obtained by applying the 38.2 percent figure for 1974 estimated in the 1976 GAO study.

57 The term "standards" is used here to mean both voluntary and mandatory requirements. In the GATT code, more precise terminology is employed. *Technical specifications* set characteristics of a product, such as quality, performance, safety, dimensions, packaging, marking or labeling, testing, or test methods. *Technical regulations* are mandatory technical specifications; *standards* are technical specifications approved by a recognized standardizing body with which compliance is voluntary. *Certification systems* and *testing methods* are technical regulations which set out procedures for determining a product's conformity with technical regulations or standards.

58 U.S. Tariff Commission, "Standards as Technical Barriers to Trade," in *Trade Barriers,* Part II, TC Publication 665 (Washington, 1974), Chapter X.

59 The Labor-Industry Coalition for International Trade, *Performance Requirements: A Study of the Incidence and Impact of Trade-Related Performance Requirements, and an Analysis of International Law* (Washington, 1981).

Domestic Production Subsidies 3

National governments subsidize domestic production through a variety of means. Subsidies may be provided directly through cash payments or indirectly with measures such as special tax deductions and credits and benefits-in-kind. The latter include the provision of goods and services to firms at below-market prices or at no cost. Governments may make materials or services available to firms and thereby subsidize their costs with tax dollars—technical assistance and export marketing subsidies are common examples. Alternatively, governments may force an industry to sell its product at below-market prices and thereby implicitly tax the regulated industry and subsidize its customers.

Subsidies may also arise from the government provision of credit at below-market interest rates. Conceptually, the subsidy element in a government direct, guaranteed or insured loan is the difference between the discounted present value of the payments required to service the loan if the loan had been obtained in the open credit market and the discounted present value of the payments required to service the loan at the concessional rate.

Further, a firm may be subsidized through public ownership or equity participation. Public enterprises are clearly subsidized when they continue to operate at a loss, due to government transfers of cash. But they are also subsidized if they operate at a below-market profit rate because the government is willing to accept a below-market or even zero return on its equity.

The United States has used many of these means, but not to the same degree as have the other AICs, to subsidize various sectors of the economy.

U.S. programs potentially affecting trade in manufactures may be divided into two groups—general programs providing benefits across many manufacturing sectors, and industry-specific programs.[1]

General assistance programs have included:

- adjustment and regional development assistance through programs administered by the Small Business Administration (SBA), the Economic Development Administration (EDA) and the Farmers Home Administration (FmHA). Aid has included direct loans, loan guarantees and insurance, and technical assistance;

- incentives for industry R&D through special tax provisions;

- benefits-in-kind subsidies through crude oil and natural gas price regulations.

Specific industries that benefit from special programs include:

- shipbuilding—Maritime Administration loans, loan guarantees and cash grants; special tax deferral programs for ship operators to renew their fleets;

- footwear—loans, loan guarantees and technical assistance administered under the Footwear Industry Revitalization Program (1977–80);

- textiles and apparel—loans, loan guarantees and technical assistance under a special Department of Commerce adjustment assistance program (1979–80);

- steel—a special $550 million loan guarantee program administered by EDA (FY 1978–79);

- automobiles—$1.2 billion in federal loan guarantees to the Chrysler Corporation (FY 1980–82).

The estimates presented in this chapter indicate that on average across the full range of manufacturing industries, the subsidy provided by these programs has been modest, only about 1 percent of the value of output in 1976. For some industries, firms and workers directly touched by these programs, however, assistance has been important. And while U.S. programs that have subsidized domestic production are similar to some of those employed by other AICs, the results presented here indicate that the aid provided by other AICs' domestic assistance programs appears to be much greater than U.S. efforts.

The remainder of this chapter is divided into three sections. The first describes general programs that benefit to some extent the full spectrum of industries, while the second section focuses on industry-specific programs. The third examines the combined effects of these programs and compares the benefits provided with those of programs in other AICs.

GENERAL PROGRAMS

(1) Adjustment Assistance to Firms and Regional Development Programs

The *Small Business Administration* offers loans, loan guarantees and management assistance to firms adversely impacted by import competition. Under Section 7(a) of the Small Business Administration Act, SBA may provide loans or loan guarantees to firms wishing to construct, expand or convert facilities; buy buildings, machinery, equipment, supplies, and materials; or raise working capital. SBA can extend a loan or guarantee for a maximum period of 10 years (20 years for real estate and construction loans).[2]

Section 502 of this act permits SBA indirectly to assist small firms by providing direct or participating loans, or guaranteeing loans, to local development companies. (Local development companies raise capital for local small business development and may be geared to assisting a particular business.) These loans and guarantees may be used to buy land, machinery and equipment, or to build, expand or convert a plant. These credits are extended for periods of 15 to 20 years.[3]

In 1976, SBA authorized about $270 million in loans and about $2 billion in loan guarantees at average interest rates of 6.7 and 9.7 percent, respectively (see Table 3-1). By 1979, loans grew to $375 million while loan guarantees increased to about $2.7 billion; the average rate of interest for loans was 8.3 percent and for loan guarantees, 11.0 percent.

TABLE 3-1. SUMMARY: MAJOR INCENTIVES TO DOMESTIC MANUFACTURING, 1975-79
($ Millions)

	1975	1976	1977	1978	1979
SBA					
Loans	$ 243.1	$ 269.7	$ 316.4	$ 332.1	$ 375.4
Loan guarantees	1,355.7	1,969.4	2,409.3	2,595.0	2,739.0
EDA					
Loans	28.8	49.3	65.1	107.7	126.7
Loan guarantees	37.4	23.6	42.1	188.4	338.7
Technical assistance	11.7	13.8	18.1	32.3	32.4
FmHA					
Loan guarantees	300.4	350.1	470.9	976.8	1,149.0
Shipbuilding					
Tax savings	90.0	87.5	117.5	78.8	75.0
Loan guarantees	752.5	728.7	848.8	559.2	980.0
Subsidies	217.6	201.2	203.3	167.3	216.9
R&D expensing	992.5	1,387.5	1,415.0	1,420.0	1,592.5
Industrial development					
bonds tax savings	200.0	257.5	326.3	450.0	598.8

Sources: SBA; EDA *(Annual Reports)*; FmHA; Maritime Administration *(Annual Reports)*; Office of Management and Budget, *Special Analysis of the Budget*, various issues; Congressional Budget Office.

Until fiscal year 1982, the *Economic Development Administration* extended financial assistance and technical assistance under the Business Development Program for economically depressed areas and the Trade Adjustment Assistance Program.

EDA's Business Development Program offered direct loans and loan guarantees to firms unable to obtain financing with long-term, low interest loans and guarantees in economically depressed areas. Title II of the Public Works and Economic Development Act (PWEDA) of 1965 authorized EDA to extend:

- fixed asset loans to purchase and develop land, to buy or build buildings and to buy and install machinery and equipment. These loans covered up to 65 percent of the total project cost for up to 25 years;

- working capital loans of not more than 7 years;

- fixed asset and working capital loan guarantees for up to 90 percent of the outstanding balance of such commercial loans. These loans were usually made for a term comparable to the life of the asset they financed.[4]

In addition to PWEDA loans and guarantees, EDA was authorized by the Trade Act of 1974 to provide trade adjustment assistance to firms and communities suffering from, or facing the threat of, severe import competition. Begun in FY 1976, low interest business loans and guarantees for up to 90 percent of the face value of the loan were available for fixed assets and working capital.[5] Firms also used EDA technical assistance to become more competitive by providing necessary training for plant modernization, improved management and marketing techniques. The trade adjustment program accounted for about 15 to 20 percent of EDA's total credit and technical assistance programs.

In 1976, EDA authorized about $49 million in direct loans and $24 million in loan guarantees and spent $14 million on technical assistance. By 1979, EDA assistance grew to $127 million in loans, $339 million in loan guarantees and $32 million in technical assistance. In 1976, the average rates of interest charged for loans and loan guarantees were 8.1 and 9.0 percent, respectively; by 1979, these rates rose to 10.5 and 12.0 percent.

Until 1982, the *Farmers Home Administration* operated a Business and Industry Development Loan Guarantee Program to assist industrial development in rural areas. FmHA guaranteed up to 90 percent of private commercial loans with maturities of 7 years (working capital) to 30 years (land, plant and equipment loans).[6] In 1976, FmHA authorized loan guarantees totaling $350 million, and in 1979 this figure grew to over $1 billion. The average interest rates charged on an FmHA loan were 9.7 percent in 1976 and 11.3 percent in 1979.[7]

Table 3-2 presents the sectoral distribution of SBA, EDA and FmHA credit authorizations and technical assistance. The distribution tends to vary from year to year, and therefore, a three-year average was computed. Such an average is more indicative of the long-run distribution of the sectoral impacts of these programs.

From 1975 to 1977, SBA, EDA and FmHA extended loans, loan guarantees and technical assistance totaling about $2.7 billion. Of this, about $750 million, or 28 percent, went to manufacturing activities—SBA provided 64 percent, EDA 9 percent and FmHA 27 percent. Of the major manufacturing sectors, those receiving greater than average assistance were:

Major Manufacturing Sector (SIC)	Assistance to Manufacturing
Machinery, except electrical (35)	13.1%
Food and kindred products (20)	12.1
Fabricated metal products (34)	8.9
Lumber and wood products (24)	8.2
Transportation equipment (37)	6.3
Electric and electronic equipment (36)	6.3
Textile mill products (22)	5.1

Table 3-3 gives sectoral estimates of the average annual rates of subsidy of EDA, SBA and FmHA credit and technical assistance programs. As discussed in Appendix C, the subsidies implicit in government direct and guaranteed loans were estimated by subtracting the discounted present value of the payments required to retire the loans from the discounted present value of the payments that would have been required had the loan been financed at the market rate.

To perform these computations, it was necessary to select a market rate of interest (r) for each fiscal year of the programs. For fiscal years 1975-77, the annual *Special Analyses of the Budget* evaluated the subsidy element of federal credit programs with an assumed market rate. For these years, the *Special Analyses* interest rates were used in this study.[8]

The estimated subsidies implicit in SBA, EDA and FmHA credit programs were added to the value of technical assistance provided by EDA and then divided by the value of each industry's output to obtain the rates of subsidy presented in the table. Without exception, the apparent subsidy impact of these programs was very small.

TABLE 3-2. SECTORAL SUMMARY OF ADJUSTMENT ASSISTANCE TO FIRMS AND REGIONAL DEVELOPMENT PROGRAM AUTHORIZATIONS, AVERAGE FOR 1975-77
($ Millions)

Major Manufacturing Sector (SIC)	SBA Credit	EDA Credit	EDA Technical Assistance	FmHA Credit	Total Programs
Food and kindred products (20)	$ 39.9	$15.0	$0.2	$ 36.0	$ 91.1
Tobacco manufactures (21)	0.5	*	—	—	0.5
Textile mill products (22)	11.5	7.9	—	19.4	38.8
Apparel and other textile products (23)	20.0	*	—	2.9	22.9
Lumber and wood products (24)	37.6	1.2	—	22.7	61.5
Furniture and fixtures (25)	20.9	2.4	—	4.0	27.3
Paper and allied products (26)	10.4	0.8	—	2.2	13.4
Printing and publishing (27)	27.5	0.2	—	1.7	29.4
Chemicals and allied products (28)	20.1	0.2	—	16.0	36.3
Petroleum and coal products (29)	2.5	*	—	1.7	4.2
Rubber and miscellaneous plastic products (30)	23.0	2.8	—	8.9	34.7
Leather and leather products (31)	5.8	7.2	—	2.0	15.0
Stone, clay and glass products (32)	22.7	3.4	—	10.5	36.6
Primary metal products (33)	14.9	9.4	—	11.2	35.5
Fabricated metal products (34)	53.2	2.3	—	11.7	67.2
Machinery (exc. electrical) (35)	71.1	2.7	—	25.4	99.2
Electric and electronic equipment (36)	37.6	4.0	—	5.8	47.4
Transportation equipment (37)	22.1	8.2	—	17.5	47.8
Instruments and related products (38)	15.9	0.5	—	1.3	17.7
Miscellaneous manufactured products (39)	22.8	1.5	—	2.4	26.7
Total manufacturing (20-39)	480.3	71.1	0.2	202.9	754.5
Total (all sectors)	2,187.9	82.1	14.5	373.8	2,658.3

*No separate breakout—included in SIC 39.
Sources: SBA; EDA; and FmHA.

To evaluate the impact of the choice of r on the estimates presented in the table, a second set of subsidy rate estimates were made with the interest rate set 2 percentage points higher (r + 2%); the results are reported in Table C-1 (Appendix C). Whether evaluated at the assumed market rate of interest or at the market rate plus 2 percentage points, these programs benefited the entire manufacturing sector with an average rate of subsidy of less than one-tenth of one percent. Furthermore, these programs did not provide any single major manufacturing sector with subsidies greater than one-tenth of one percent. Therefore, while SBA, EDA and FmHA programs may have had important consequences for individual communities and firms assisted, their impacts on the overall structure of U.S. industry and trade were hardly noticeable.

Under President Reagan's economic program, the benefits provided by SBA, EDA and FmHA have been reduced. The 1983 budget indicated that in FY 1982, SBA loans would be about $184 million (one-half their 1979 level) and SBA loan guarantees would be about $2.7 billion, which is about the same as in 1979. After 1982, under Administration plans, new business development and trade adjustment assistance loans and loan guarantees will not be available from EDA and FmHA, and EDA is being phased out altogether. Overall, these measures should reduce the subsidy provided manufacturing by SBA, EDA and FmHA in 1982 to about one-half the 1979 amount.[9]

TABLE 3-3. DOMESTIC PRODUCTION SUBSIDIES, 1976
(Percent)

Major Manufacturing Sector (SIC)	EDA, SBA and FmHA[1]	R&D	Petroleum	Shipbuilding	Total Domestic Production Subsidies
Food and kindred products (20)	0.0013	0.0011[2]	0.0571	—	0.0595
Tobacco manufactures (21)	0.0009	0.0011[2]	0.0219	—	0.0239
Textile mill products (22)	0.0034	0.0011[2]	0.0893	—	0.0938
Apparel and other textile products (23)	0.0024	0.0011[2]	0.0438	—	0.0473
Lumber and wood products (24)	0.0036	0.0103	0.3125	—	0.3264
Furniture and fixtures (25)	0.0055	0.0206	0.0846	—	0.1107
Paper and allied products (26)	0.0008	0.0011[2]	0.2213	—	0.2232
Printing and publishing (27)	0.0021	0.0011[2]	0.0508	—	0.0540
Chemicals and allied products (28)	0.0006	0.1559	0.1978	—	0.3543
Petroleum and coal products (29)	0.0008	0.0361	0.0593[3]	—	0.0962
Rubber and miscellaneous plastic products (30)	0.0026	0.0011[2]	0.0740	—	0.0777
Leather and leather products (31)	0.0114	0.0114	0.0846	—	0.1074
Stone, clay and glass products (32)	0.0003	0.0011[2]	0.2163	—	0.2177
Primary metal products (33)	0.0010	0.0283	0.1040	—	0.1333
Fabricated metal products (34)	0.0020	0.0252	0.0784	—	0.1056
Machinery (exc. electrical) (35)	0.0021	0.1685	0.1177	—	0.2883
Electric and electronic equipment (36)	0.0015	0.2555	0.0619	—	0.3189
Transportation equipment (37)	0.0006	0.1599	0.0577	0.2795	0.4977
Shipbuilding (3731)				5.2879	
Instruments and related products (38)	0.0014	0.2775	0.0889	—	0.3678
Miscellaneous manufactured products (39)	0.0049	0.0011	0.1742	—	0.1802
Total manufacturing (20–39)	0.0015	0.0808	0.0995	0.0322	0.2140

1 A subsidy is the sum of an average of all program subsidies for 1975–77.
2 This category is included in Miscellaneous manufactured products.
3 Positive value in this sector reflects inclusion of nonpetroleum refining activities.
Source: Authors' estimates.

(2) Tax Incentives for R&D

The federal government encourages R&D through direct expenditures and tax incentives.

Direct expenditures support two types of R&D. First, the government purchases R&D as part of its provision of public goods and services—e.g., national defense and environmental protection. In these cases, it is the sole or primary initial user of discoveries and innovations.

Second, support is provided when the federal government believes that certain R&D expenditures are in the national interest but that the private sector is unlikely to undertake them because the benefits, in large measure, are not immediately realized by the firm. Such R&D would include various basic, agricultural and health sciences research. In these areas, the social benefits are greater than the private costs of undertaking the R&D expenditures, but the private benefits are less than the private costs; R&D becomes a public good much like public education.

Undoubtedly, federal expenditures on R&D improve the international competitive position of many U.S. industries. But to the extent that government finances R&D as part of the process of providing public-sector goods and services or R&D that would not normally be undertaken by the private sector, such support is not trade distorting, as the concept was defined in Chapter 1. The problem emerges when the government finances all or part of private R&D that would be undertaken by private firms in the absence of government support. However, this is not the federal government's intention nor is it likely often to be the case.[10]

The federal government also supports private-sector R&D through tax incentives. Firms are permitted to deduct the full cost of capital equipment used to undertake R&D when incurred, instead of depreciating the equipment over its useful life. This benefit is provided to all firms regardless of whether a national interest is at stake. Such subsidies may be viewed as affecting trade.[11]

The Office of Management and Budget estimated that this provision generated for firms the following tax savings, which represent a substantial share of company R&D expenditures:[12]

	Tax Savings ($ Millions)	Share of Company R&D
1975	992.5	6.38%
1976	1,387.5	7.98
1977	1,415.0	7.29
1978	1,420.0	6.43
1979	1,592.5	n.a.
1980	1,860.0	n.a.

These tax expenditures are most likely distributed among firms and industries according to their shares of private-sector expenditures for R&D. Table 3-4 reports the sectoral distribution of company expenditures on R&D. The major manufacturing sectors accounting for the largest shares of these expenditures from 1975 to 1978 were transportation equipment (SIC 37), electric and electronic equipment (36), machinery, except electrical (35), and petrochemicals (28).

TABLE 3-4. COMPANY R&D FUNDS, 1975-78
($ Millions)

Major Manufacturing Sector (SIC)	1975	1976	1977	1978
Tobacco manufactures (21)	[1]	[1]	72	87
Lumber and wood products (24)	46	59	76	83
Furniture and fixtures (25)	43	47	50	54
Chemicals and allied products (28)	2,490	2,751	2,956	3,232
Petroleum and coal products (29)	[1]	715	842	952
Leather and leather products (31)	11	13	12	13
Primary metal products (33)	422	481	507	518
Fabricated metal products (34)	297	322	349	360
Machinery (exc. electrical) (35)	2,687	2,955	3,391	3,875
Electric and electronic equipment (36)	2,798	3,081	3,238	3,769
Transportation equipment (37)	3,344	3,853	4,520	[1]
Instruments and related products (38)	1,007	1,144	1,313	1,529
Miscellaneous manufactured products[2] (39)	76	84	91	101
Total manufacturing (20-39)	15,271	16,905	18,899	21,504
Total (all sectors)	15,559	17,377	19,407	22,098

1 This category is included in Miscellaneous manufactured products.
2 This category is composed of SICs 20-23, 26, 27, 30, and 32.
Source: National Science Foundation, *Research and Development in Industry, Technical Notes and Detailed Statistical Tables*, Table B-2, various issues.

The subsidy rates for major manufacturing sectors in 1976 were estimated by allocating to each sector the tax savings for that year based on the sectoral distribution of company R&D expenditures and then dividing these tax savings by each sector's 1976 output. As Table 3-3 shows, the estimated subsidy accruing to the entire manufacturing sector was about 0.1 percent. However, the subsidy rates were significantly higher for the five sectors responsible for the largest shares of company R&D funds:

Major Manufacturing Sectors (SIC)	Subsidy Rate
Instruments and related products (38)	0.3%
Electric and electronic equipment (36)	0.3
Machinery, except electrical (35)	0.2
Transportation equipment (37)	0.2
Chemicals and allied products (28)	0.2

The tax cut passed by Congress in August 1981 includes a provision to extend the tax benefits for R&D to incorporate tax credits for qualified operating expenses — e.g., wages, supplies and leasing computers.[13] The provisions should augment the benefits received from the capital write-off provision by about 15 percent in 1982 and 20 percent in 1986.

(3) Crude Oil and Natural Gas Price Regulations

The crude oil price regulations in place from 1971 to 1981 functioned much like a tax on domestic crude oil producers whose revenues were used to subsidize other industries and domestic consumers.

When price controls were initiated in 1971, virtually all petroleum product prices were regulated, and most of the benefits of crude oil price regulations were passed on to firms using petroleum products as material inputs and to final consumers.

In 1976, refiners' average acquisition costs for all crude oil (domestic and imported) was only about 81 percent of the average acquisition cost of imported crude oil alone ($13.48 per barrel).[14] This created a $2.59 subsidy on each barrel of crude oil converted to petroleum products. To the extent that petroleum price regulations and competition assured that this benefit was passed on to users of petroleum products, firms in the manufacturing sector received a subsidy equal to about $1.2 billion or about 0.1 percent of the value of manufactured products produced.[15]

The subsidy rates accruing to individual sectors were estimated by allocating the total subsidy ($1.2 billion) among the manufacturing sectors according to their shares of petroleum product consumption (see Table 5-2).[16] The major manufacturing sectors receiving the largest subsidies were:

Major Manufacturing Sector (SIC)	Subsidy Rate
Lumber and wood products (24)	0.31%
Paper and allied products (26)	0.22
Stone, clay and glass products (32)	0.22
Chemicals and allied products (28)	0.20
Miscellaneous manufactures (39)	0.17

In 1976, 1979 and 1980, many petroleum product prices were deregulated, and competition among refiners over this period became increasingly significant in assuring that the benefits of crude oil price regulations were passed on to refinery customers.[17] All of these rates of subsidy are less than 1 percent, but they tell only part of the story. Many sectors also benefit from natural gas price regulations. For the 1970s, the analysis that follows indicates that the combined benefits of petroleum and natural gas price controls were several times greater than the benefits from petroleum price controls alone.

Estimating the subsidies to manufacturing by natural gas price regulations is much more difficult than for the case of crude oil price regulations. First, natural gas prices have been regulated to some degree since 1954, and imports only contribute less than 5 percent to total supply. At least until recently, price regulations have depressed exploration for new gas and the domestic supply while encouraging the use of natural gas in place of other fuels. It is very difficult to say what the domestic price of natural gas would be today in the absence of so many years of regulation. Unlike crude oil, there is no reference price against which current prices can be compared with confidence to estimate the subsidy provided consumers by price controls. Second, the price paid for natural gas by industrial users varies considerably among firms and industries.

Therefore, estimates of the benefits received by individual industrial sectors are difficult to make and is a task beyond the scope of this study.

To give some indication of the magnitude of the subsidy involved, the average price of all natural gas (both imported and domestic) as it entered the U.S. distribution system was compared with the average price of imported natural gas. This probably provides a conservative estimate because the average price of imported natural gas does not reflect the marginal cost of adding imports to natural gas, owing to the effects of long-term contracts, the prices of which have been depressed by price controls in earlier years. Furthermore, the average price of imported gas is considerably less than the price of imported oil on a Btu equivalent basis:

	Price per 1000 Cu. Ft.[18]	
	1976	1979
Average sale price of domestic and imported gas together	$0.584	$1.357
Average price of imported gas alone	1.727	2.601
Cost of Btu equivalent imported oil	2.520	4.028

The manufacturing sector purchased an estimated 7.9 billion cubic feet in 1976 and 7.2 billion cubic feet in 1979. If the average prices paid for natural gas in the absence of price controls had been equal to the average price of imported gas, then price regulations created average subsidies on each 1000 cubic feet purchased equal to about $1.14 in 1976 and $1.24 in 1979. On this basis, the estimated subsidy to the manufacturing sector was equal to $9.1 billion, or 0.7 percent of the value of manufactured shipments, about seven times larger than the estimated subsidy created by crude oil price regulations. In 1979, the subsidy was $8.9 billion, or about 0.6 percent of the value of manufactured shipments.

Under the Natural Gas Policy Act of 1978 (NGPA), the price of *new sources* of natural gas will be deregulated in 1985. Since consumers pay average prices, the continued control of "old gas" will create an ongoing subsidy for natural gas users for many years. A 1981 American Oil Company study projected gas prices (in 1981 dollars) for 1985 under alternative regulatory scenarios.[19] According to the study, with complete decontrol, the price of natural gas would be $5.40 per 1000 cubic feet, and with continued controls under the NGPA, $3.90 per 1000 cubic feet. Hence, continued controls would imply a projected subsidy of $1.50 per cubic foot. Under continued controls, industrial users would be expected to purchase 6.9 billion cubic feet and receive a subsidy of about $10.4 billion dollars. If the manufacturing sector continued to account for 93.3 percent of industrial use, it would receive a subsidy equal to $9.7 billion. Accounting for expected growth in the manufacturing sector, this implies a subsidy of about 0.4 percent of the value of manufactured shipments.

For the reasons cited in Appendix C, it was not possible to allocate the subsidy provided by natural gas price regulations across manufacturing sectors. However, industries using natural gas intensively probably gain the most from price regulations. They include primary metals (especially iron and steel); stone, glass and clay products; and petrochemicals. The latter includes sectors employing natural gas and petroleum directly—organic chemicals, nitrogenous fertilizer and carbon black—and their customers—e.g., plastics, synthetic rubber and synthetic fibers.

(4) Industrial Revenue Bonds

Firms in both the industrial and nonindustrial sectors may obtain below-market financing through industrial revenue bonds. IRBs are tax exempt,[20] typically issued by a local government, whose proceeds are used to buy a facility or equipment. A firm then buys these on installments or leases them.

Essentially, IRBs permit firms to borrow at below-market rates because of their tax-exempt status. During 1979, IRBs were usually issued at fixed interest rates between 6.5 and 10.0 percent, depending on the type of project and the creditworthiness of the borrower. But by the end of that year, as interest rates soared, IRBs were issued at floating rates of between 8.75 and 9.5 percent (in general, 55–75 percent of the prime rate) and the loan term was shortened from as long as 25 years in 1978 to about 10 years.

The Office of Management and Budget estimated that IRBs cost the federal government $258 million in foregone tax revenue in 1976 (see Table 3-1). This cost is estimated to reach $2.2 billion in FY 1983.

These savings accrue to a wide variety of firms, some manufacturing and some less traditional users, including shopping centers, grocery stores, private sports clubs, hotels, and health facilities. A small portion of IRBs (those sold publicly) are reported by the *Daily Bond Buyer*[21]; the value of these bonds sold for industrial purposes increased steadily since 1976, reaching $1.3 billion in 1979:

	Bond Value ($ Millions)
1976	356.9
1977	463.8
1978	586.1
1979	1,339.9

However, because privately issued IRBs are generally not officially recorded,[22] it is difficult to measure the actual total volume of IRBs issued as well as the sectoral distribution of the users. Nevertheless, through the use of surveys, the CBO attempted to make a rough determination of the volume and users of IRBs. It found that manufacturing firms and national retail and fast food chains have used IRBs to finance major expansion programs. In addition, it found that large IRB users are manufacturers of food products, household products, textiles, chemicals, and pulp and paper.[23]

INDUSTRY-SPECIFIC PROGRAMS

The federal government has offered special programs to meet the specific needs of several manufacturing sectors: shipbuilding, footwear, textiles and apparel, and automobiles.

(1) Shipbuilding

Credit programs, special tax incentives and direct subsidy payments are extended to assist the U.S. shipbuilding industry.

The Maritime Administration guarantees loans to finance the construction or reconstruction of U.S. flag vessels in domestic shipyards. Through the Federal Ship Financing Program, private-sector loans to U.S. shipowners are guaranteed for periods up to 25 years. In 1976, loan guarantees were $729 million, and the average interest rate was 7.5 percent. In 1978, these loan guarantees fell to $559 million with an average interest rate of 8.6 percent, but rose again in 1979 to $980 million with an average interest rate of 9.7 percent (see Table 3-1).

Tax incentives are provided to U.S. citizens owning or leasing vessels through the Capital Construction Fund (CCF) and the Construction Reserve Fund (CRF). Federal taxes are deferred on money deposited into these funds and on money withdrawn to construct vessels in U.S. shipyards. Taxes may be deferred indefinitely as long as the money initially deposited in these funds is reinvested in vessels constructed in U.S. shipyards.

Any U.S. flag operator of a vessel engaged in domestic or international commerce or in fishing may establish a CCF with the Secretary of Commerce. He may deposit all or a portion of income earned from the operation of his vessel, the capital gains from the sale of his vessel, and the earnings from the investment or reinvestment of amounts on deposit in the fund. The operator may use the funds placed in the CCF, as well as accumulated investment earnings, to buy, construct, or reconstruct vessels and certain related equipment in U.S. shipyards and factories, or to repay mortgages on U.S. vessels. As long as he plans to replace or expand his fleet of vessels, the operator can extend the CCF tax deferrals indefinitely.

The Construction Reserve Fund is a second tax deferral program for U.S. shipowners authorized by the amended Merchant Marine Act of 1936. Using the CRF, shipowners operating vessels in foreign and domestic commerce may defer federal income taxes on the proceeds from the sale or loss of a vessel, provided these proceeds are used to construct, reconstruct or purchase a new vessel within three years. Because the benefits of the CRF program are somewhat similar to, but not as broad as, the benefits of the CCF program, CRF is predominantly used by ship operators on inland waterways or in other trades not eligible for the CCF.

The tax savings created by the CCF and CRF fluctuated over the 1975-78 period, from a low of $79 million in 1978 to a high of $118 million in 1977 (see Table 3-1).

Finally, to place U.S. shipbuilding construction, reconstruction and reconditioning costs on a par with foreign construction costs, the federal government provides Construction Differential Subsidies to U.S. shipbuilders. These grants are equal to the difference in the cost of constructing a ship in a domestic rather than a foreign shipyard and may not exceed 50 percent of the domestic cost. These CDSs are available to any U.S. citizen, and ships must be suitable for national defense purposes and be operated by U.S. citizens. If a ship is used for domestic trade, a portion of the CDS must be refunded. Since 1975, annual outlays for these subsidies have fluctuated between $167 million and $218 million (see Table 3-1).

For 1975-77, the estimated subsidies provided by loan guarantees, tax deferrals and cash subsidies to domestic shipbuilders are presented in Table 3-5. The subsidies extended by Maritime Administration loans were estimated in the same way as those implicit in SBA, EDA and FmHA loans. The rates of subsidy provided the shipbuilding

TABLE 3-5. SHIPBUILDING INCENTIVE PROGRAMS, 1975-77

	1975	1976	1977	Average 1975-77
Subsidy amount ($ millions)				
Loan guarantees	$ 84.8	$ 79.7	$147.7	$104.1
Tax savings[1]	90.0	87.5	117.5	98.3
Cash subsidies[2]	217.6	201.2	203.3	207.4
Total	392.4	368.4	468.5	409.8
Rate of subsidy (percent)				
Loan guarantees	1.19%	1.05%	1.72%	1.32%
Tax savings[1]	1.27	1.16	1.37	1.27
Cash subsidies[2]	3.06	2.66	2.37	2.70
Total	5.52	4.87	5.46	5.29

1 OMB estimate of the tax savings provided by the CCF and the CRF.
2 CDS.
Source: Authors' estimates.

industry by these programs were obtained by dividing these subsidies by the value of shipbuilding production. The total estimated rate of subsidy received by shipbuilders was 5.5 percent in 1975, 4.9 percent in 1976 and 5.5 percent in 1977. Fluctuations in the value of loan guarantee authorizations were responsible for most of the year-to-year variations in the overall rate of subsidy. Over the period, the average subsidy was 5.3 percent, which is the highest rate of subsidy received by any of the industries reported in this chapter. However, it is important to keep in mind that in many other countries, shipbuilding has been, at least until recently, one of the more heavily subsidized and protected industries.

Under President Reagan's economic program, the benefits received by the shipbuilding industry will decline dramatically. According to the 1983 budget, the President plans to reduce the loan guarantee limit from $1 billion in 1981 to $675 million in 1982 and to $600 million in 1983 and to hold Construction Differential Subsidies to $100 million a year from 1983 to 1985, about one-half their 1979 level. These actions are estimated to reduce the rate of subsidy received by the shipbuilding industry from 5.5 percent in 1977 to 4.7 and 2.4 percent in 1982 and 1985, respectively.

(2) Footwear

To revitalize the footwear industry and improve its international competitiveness, a three-year trade adjustment assistance program was begun in 1977. Three divisions of the Department of Commerce (the EDA, the Office of Productivity, Technology and Innovation, and the International Trade Administration) set up the Footwear Industry Revitalization Program with $56 million in funding for loans, loan guarantees, technical and managerial assistance, and export promotion efforts. The primary thrust of FIRP was technical assistance. In the past, footwear firms were eager to avail themselves of EDA trade adjustment assistance loans and loan guarantees (see the earlier section on "General Programs"); however, because policymakers within the government felt that "technical and managerial assistance when combined with loans or loan guarantees is more likely to result in effective economic adjustment than financed assistance alone,"[24] EDA's financial trade adjustment assistance programs were combined with enhanced technical assistance in FIRP. In addition, the program was intended to operate in conjunction with the four-year orderly marketing agreements discussed in Chapter 2.

By April 1980, 52 footwear firms had received $57.7 million in loans and loan guarantees, exhausting the program's budget. In addition, $5.9 million was spent on technical assistance projects over the same period (see Table 3-6). FIRP was terminated in April 1980.

The Commerce Department estimated the benefits realized by the footwear industry from the technical assistance of FIRP during the first two years of the program.[25] Stressing the preliminary nature of their results (which were based on only 18 of the more than 60 technical assistance projects in operation at the end of the second year of the program), Commerce concluded that FIRP technical assistance reduced costs, increased productivity and improved factory methods.

Commerce estimated that technical assistance aspects of FIRP resulted in annual cost savings equal to $4.4 million a year (see Table 3-7); this was about 0.1 percent of 1979 industry output. The terms of FIRP loan guarantees were not publicly

TABLE 3-6. ALLOCATION OF FOOTWEAR INDUSTRY REVITALIZATION PROGRAM ASSISTANCE, 1977-80
($ Thousands)

	1977[1]	1978	1979	1980[2]
Loans and loan guarantees	$7,985	$4,224	$43,775	$1,750
Technical assistance[3]	158	2,941	2,698	54
Total	8,195	8,145	47,372	1,822

1 July 20, 1977 to January 20, 1978.
2 January 20, 1980 to April 20, 1980.
3 These funds reflect the government's share of technical assistance funding. A total of $8 million was spent on technical assistance over the course of the program, but $2 million of that was contributed by footwear manufacturers.
Source: Department of Commerce, *Footwear Industry Revitalization Program, 1980*, Annual Progress Report, pp. 2-3.

TABLE 3-7. ESTIMATED ANNUAL SAVINGS TO FOOTWEAR INDUSTRY FROM TECHNICAL ASSISTANCE, 1977-80
($ Thousands)

Production costs	$ 186.0
Materials utilization	1,127.7
Elimination of inventory loss	425.0
Improvements in productivity and factory operation	2,142.6
Savings passed on to employees	190.9
Reduction in sales expense	305.0
Overhead absorption	56.5
Total	$4,433.7

Source: Department of Commerce, *Footwear Industry Revitalization Program, 1980*, Annual Progress Report, p. 13.

available, so the subsidy implicit in these credits could not be estimated in the same way as have the other federal credit programs. However, it is apparent that these loans were important. The $58 million loaned was considerably greater than the footwear industry's annual capital expenditures prior to the program—about $32 million in 1976 and 1977. If the annual subsidy over the life of the loans was 5 percent of their value, then the loan guarantees provided the industry with an annual subsidy equal to $2.9 million, or 0.06 percent of 1979 industry output.

Moreover, while separate data on the terms of FIRP loans and loan guarantees are not available, the value of the credits, as well as FIRP technical assistance, are included in the values of EDA credits and technical assistance reported in Tables 3-1 and 3-2, in the estimated rates of subsidy for the leather products industry reported in Table 3-3, and the estimated rates of subsidy to all manufacturing by EDA reported in Table 3-8.

(3) Other Programs

Steel

In March 1978, EDA set up a special loan guarantee program to assist medium-size steel producers adversely affected by changes in market conditions, foreign competition and a shortage of capital required for plant modernization and pollution abatement. EDA was authorized to guarantee up to $500 million of private-sector loans; by the end of 1980, EDA had approved guarantees totaling just over $360 million ($21.3 million in 1978, $343.3 million in 1979 and none since 1979).

The amount of loan guarantees available under this program is small compared to the capital needs of the industry. While the subsidies implicit in low interest guaranteed loans were important to the five firms receiving this assistance, the impact on the entire industry is very small. And the long-term impact of the program on U.S. imports is probably not very noticeable.

Textiles and Apparel

In 1979, the Commerce Department, through EDA, undertook a special trade adjustment assistance program for the textile and apparel industry, with three main components:

- a Productivity Improvement Program providing grants for research, employee training and other projects designed to encourage the application of new technologies and market expansion;

- increased EDA financial and technical assistance for firms; in 1979, loans and loan guarantees totaling $23 million and technical assistance costing $1.5 million were provided;

- an export expansion program.

Automobiles

During the 1970s, Chrysler's market share dropped from 16 percent to 9 percent. As profits fell, cash-flow problems necessitated some liquidation of assets, and the firm experienced losses of $205 million in 1978 and $1.1 billion in 1979.

The cash-flow drain occurred at the same time substantial capital was needed to finance modernization and the down-sizing required to meet government fuel and

TABLE 3-8. SUMMARY OF PROTECTION EXTENDED BY DOMESTIC PRODUCTION SUBSIDIES, 1976 (ESTIMATED), 1982 AND 1985 (PROJECTED)
(Percent)

	1976	1982	1985
EDA, SBA, FmHA	0.0015	0.0008[a]	0.0008[a]
R&D	0.0808	0.1107[b]	0.1165[b]
Petroleum price regulations	0.0995	0	0
Natural gas price regulations	0.7303	n.a.	0.4067[c]
Shipbuilding	0.0322[d]	0.0284[d]	0.0148[d]
Chrysler	—	0.2523[e]	—
Total	0.9433	n.a.	0.5388

a This assumes a 50 percent reduction in the subsidies offered by these programs (see text).

b The rate of subsidy rose to 0.0967 percent in 1977. The 1982 and 1985 projections assume benefits from existing tax shelters remain unchanged and that the additional tax credits add 14.5 percent to benefits in 1982 and 20.5 percent in 1985.

c In 1981 dollars, the projected difference between the regulated and unregulated prices cited in the text is $1.50 per 1000 cubic feet. The American Oil Company study estimates that by 1985 industrial consumption will decline 10.2 percent from its 1979 level and therefore be 6.919 trillion cubic feet. This implies a subsidy to industry of $10.4 billion (1981 dollars) and to manufacturing of $9.7 billion (1981 dollars). Inflating to 1985 dollars using the projections in the 1983 budget, this subsidy becomes $13.4 billion. Dividing by projected manufacturing shipments for 1985 (1980 shipments reported in the *Survey of Current Business* multiplied by the nominal GNP growth rates projected in the 1983 budget) yields a projected subsidy rate equal to 0.41 percent.

d For 1975-77, the average subsidy provided shipbuilding was 5.29 percent; shipbuilding was 0.61 percent of 1976 manufacturing output: $0.0332 = (5.2879)(0.0061)$.
The subsidies to shipbuilding in FY 1978-79 were:

	Amount	Rate
	($ Mil)	(%)
Tax savings	77.5	0.84
Loan guarantees	356.2	3.88
Direct subsidies	178.5	1.94

Assuming the same rate of inflation as projected in the FY 1983 budget, the real value of the projected tax savings, loan guarantees and direct subsidies are expected to change between FY 1978/79, and FY 1982 and FY 1985 as follows:

	Percent Change	
	1978/79-82	1978/79-85
Tax savings	−23.1%	−33.7%
Loan guarantees	−22.9	−70.5
Direct subsidies	−47.9	−62.7

The projected rates of subsidy for 1982 and 1985 are:

	1982	1985
Tax savings	0.65%	0.56%
Loan guarantees	2.99	1.14
Direct subsidies	1.01	0.72
Total	4.65	2.42

These rates of subsidy for 1982 and 1985 were multiplied by shipbuilding's share of manufactured output, 0.0061, to obtain the entries in the table for 1982 and 1985.

e This assumes survival of Chrysler with a market share of at least 7.3 percent from domestic production. The tariff equivalent benefit of the Chrysler program discussed in the text (3.1 percent) was multiplied by the automobile industry's share of total 1977 manufacturing output (8.14 percent) to obtain the figure in the table.
Source: Authors' estimates.

safety regulations. In addition, a worldwide slump in demand for large cars, Chrysler's mainstay, created significant unemployment throughout the motor vehicle industry, and particularly for Chrysler.

To avoid heavy unemployment concentrated in an already depressed region, the consequent failure of small suppliers, and the heavy costs bankruptcy would have imposed on the federal government (e.g., revenue losses, unemployment claims and welfare costs), the government agreed to provide Chrysler with a $1.5 billion loan guarantee. In exchange for the guarantee, Chrysler was required to seek another $1.5 billion from other sources:

- wage concessions totaling $462.6 million from unionized labor;
- wage concessions of $125 million from nonunionized labor;
- $500 million from U.S. banks in new nonguaranteed loans and concessions on existing loans;
- $150 million from foreign banks and other financial institutions;
- $250 million from state and local governments;
- $180 million from dealers and suppliers;
- $300 million from the disposition of Chrysler assets;
- $50 million from the sale of additional equity securities.

As of July 1981, Chrysler had drawn on $1.2 billion in federal loan guarantees and does not plan to use any of the remaining guarantee funds.

It is difficult to assess the subsidy content of the guaranteed loans per se because, without federal guarantees, Chrysler would not have been able to obtain credit at any price, and these loans triggered additional assistance from other sources. However, the effect of the overall package may be evaluated in terms of estimates of the additional imports that would have resulted had Chrysler shut down.

In 1980, Chrysler's market share (excluding captive imports) was 7.3 percent, while other domestic manufacturers and import market shares were 67.5 and 25.2 percent, respectively. Had Chrysler shut down and its 1980 market share been divided among domestic producers and imports in proportion to their 1980 market shares, imports would have been 7.3 percent greater. The estimated equivalent tariff that would have restrained imports by the same amount is 3.1 percent.[26]

OVERVIEW

Table 3-8 shows the estimated average rates of subsidy provided the entire manufacturing sector by the various programs analyzed in this chapter. Overall, the programs' benefits were estimated to be the equivalent of 0.9 percent of the value of output in 1976. The general adjustment assistance and regional development programs contributed little to this total, while the benefits from petroleum and natural gas price regulations, conservatively estimated, accounted for about 88 percent. Just under 1 percent is quite small compared to the 4.9 percent protection provided by tariffs. Moreover, the benefits received by manufacturing from these programs will decline as a result of initiatives taken by the Reagan Administration.

Outlook for 1985

Budget data were employed to project the rates of subsidy implicit in the programs examined in this chapter to 1985. The combined effects of President Reagan's budget reductions and the deregulation of petroleum and natural gas prices will reduce the total estimated subsidy from just under 1 percent in 1976 to about 0.5 percent in 1985 (see Table 3-8). Petroleum and natural gas price deregulation will be responsible for most of this. Once these regulations are completely phased out, U.S. trading partners will have little to complain about in terms of the trade-distorting effects of U.S. federal subsidies to domestic industry, with the possible exception of the unestimatable effects of industrial revenue bonds.

Comparison with Other AICs

The above results are not surprising, as the United States does far less to subsidize economic activity than other major industrial countries.

For 1976, Table 3-9 shows current account subsidies and aid to capital formation in the seven major industrial countries as shares of GNP. Current account subsidies consist of grants to private and public enterprises, including payments to cover the operating losses of public corporations. Aids to private capital formation include direct grants and credits. For these forms of assistance, the United States ranks last.

However, these measures do not include several other important types of subsidies that may be used to encourage domestic production:

- the provision of goods and services at below-market prices through price controls or other means;

- special tax benefits to particular firms or for particular activities;

- implicit subsidies to public enterprises permitted to earn positive but below-market rates of return.

TABLE 3-9. PUBLIC ASSISTANCE TO ENTERPRISES IN SEVEN MAJOR INDUSTRIAL COUNTRIES, 1976
(As a Percent of GNP)

	Current Account	Capital Formation*	Total
United States	0.3	0.1	0.4
Canada	1.7	0.9	2.6
France	2.7	0.6	3.3
W. Germany	1.5	0.3	1.5
Italy	2.6	1.1	2.7
Japan	1.3	0.1	1.4
United Kingdom	2.8	0.9	3.7

*This category includes only assistance to private capital formation.
Source: John Mutti, *Taxes, Subsidies and Competitiveness Internationally* (Washington: NPA Committee on Changing International Realities, 1982).
Addenda: Value of subsidy to all U.S. industry of crude oil and natural gas price regulations: 1976, 0.7 percent; 1979, 0.6 percent. Value of tax subsidies for R&D and shipbuilding as a percent of GNP: 1976, 0.1 percent; 1979, 0.1 percent.

With respect to the first of these, the principal assistance provided U.S. industry by price controls has been crude oil and natural gas price regulations. But it is not clear that the benefits received by U.S. industry from these regulations should be included in aggregate (economywide) comparisons, such as the one presented in Table 3-9, for two reasons. First, the benefits received by agriculture, mining, construction, manufacturing, utilities, and services sectors from crude oil and natural gas price regulations were obtained at the expense of the crude oil and natural gas producers. This means that price regulations implicitly taxed one sector of the economy to subsidize the others. Second, it is not clear to what extent the benefits from price regulations ultimately reached all sectors of the economy. Nevertheless, even if the estimated value of the subsidies implicit in crude oil and natural gas price regulations and the benefits from tax laws discussed in this chapter are added to the other benefits received by U.S. industry (see column 4 of Table 3-9), without adding the comparable benefits provided by other AICs, the United States still ranks last:

	Benefits to Enterprises (As a Percent of GNP)
United States	1.2
Canada	2.6
France	3.3
W. Germany	1.5
Italy	2.7
Japan	1.4
United Kingdom	3.7

Further, the lack of data for subsidies to public enterprises when they are permitted to earn a positive but below-market rate of return almost certainly reduces the reported disparity between the United States and other AICs because the United States has few public enterprises. Unlike the other industrial countries, the United States is not inclined to establish public corporations in poorly performing industries or firms to maintain employment or achieve other national policy objectives.

It may be argued that estimates of public assistance to business, such as those presented in Table 3-9, while useful, do not present a complete picture of government involvement because levels of taxation are equally important. In particular, if taxes on business are higher or the same in countries that provide higher subsidies, the effects of taxes and subsidies could cancel out.

John Mutti, in the CIR study cited in Table 3-9, addressed this question. He estimated the net benefits to private enterprises and publicly held corporations by government spending and tax policies. A summary of his results is presented in Table 3-10. The benefits include public outlays of current account subsidies to private and public enterprises, public capital consumption, aid to private capital formation and research and development, and an estimate of the subsidy implicit in official export financing. From these benefits, Mutti subtracted corporate income taxes. According to this measure of assistance to industry, the United States ranks last. While it is important to remember that these estimates provide only an approximate measure of the net benefits received from various governments' tax and subsidy policies, the dispari-

TABLE 3-10. NET BENEFITS TO PRIVATE AND PUBLIC ENTERPRISES IN THE MAJOR AICS, 1976
(As a Percent of GNP)

	Benefits	Corporate Taxes	Net Benefits
United States	3.8	3.0	0.8
Canada	5.4	3.8	1.6
France	6.3	2.3	4.0
W. Germany	3.7	1.7	2.0
Italy	6.5	2.2	4.3
Japan	4.9	3.5	1.4
United Kingdom	9.3	1.7	7.6

Source: John Mutti, *Taxes, Subsidies and Competitiveness Internationally* (Washington: NPA Committee on Changing International Realities, 1982).

ty between the estimated net benefits provided by the United States and the other major AICs is striking. These results strongly suggest that U.S. domestic subsidies to industry distort trade less than the subsidies extended to industry by other major industrial countries.

Notes

1   All data in this chapter are for calendar years, unless specifically noted as fiscal years. Prior to FY 1976, fiscal years ran from July of the previous year through June of the current year. FY 1976 ran from July 1975 through June 1976. After a transition quarter from July 1976 through September 1976, fiscal years covered October of the previous year through September of the current year.

2   U.S. Congress, Joint Economic Committee, Subcommittee on Priorities and Economy in Government, *Federal Subsidy Programs,* Joint Committee Print, 93rd Congress, 2nd Session (Washington, October 18, 1974), p. 125; U.S Congress, House of Representatives, Committee on Banking, Finance and Urban Affairs, Subcommittee on Economic Stabilization, *Catalog of Federal Loan Guarantee Programs,* Committee Print, 95th Congress, First Session (Washington, September 1977), p. 196.

3   Congress, House of Representatives, *Catalog,* p. 298.

4   EDA, *1980 Annual Report,* p. 12.

5   Ibid.

6   Municipal Bond Advisers of America, *Sourceguide for Borrowing Capital* (1976), pp. 128-130.

7   The figure 11.3 percent is for FY 1979, October 1, 1978 to September 1, 1979.

8   The assumed market rate for FY 1975 was 9.5 percent and for FYs 1976 and 1977, 10 percent. For subsequent years, the *Special Analyses* presented estimates based on a range of interest rates.

9   Over the 1975-77 period, SBA, EDA and FmHA credit and technical assistance programs provided subsidy rates to manufacturing equal to 0.0009, 0.0003 and 0.0002 percent, respectively. From 1975-77 to 1982, SBA direct loans were projected in the 1983 budget to decline $83 million to $184 million; SBA loan guarantees were expected to grow from $1,586 million to $2,735 million. Over this period, overall SBA financing was projected to increase by about 57.5 percent, while GNP was expected to grow 85.6 percent. So the relative importance of SBA loans

and loan guarantees was projected to decline by about 15 percent. Assuming the subsidy to manufacturing declines proportionately, the estimated subsidy provided by SBA should have declined by about 15 percent to 0.0008 percent.

EDA's Business Development Program accounted for 80–85 percent of EDA's subsidy rate. Therefore, phasing out this program likely reduced EDA's subsidy rate to less than 0.001 percent by 1982.

Overall, the subsidy offered manufacturing by these programs likely declined from about 0.0015 to 0.0008 percent or about 50 percent. Of course, if the credits in remaining programs were made available at more attractive interest rates (in comparison to prevailing market rates of interest), the reduction in benefits may not be as large.

10   The federal government's objectives in funding R&D are outlined in Office of Management and Budget, *Special Analysis K of the Budget of the United States Government, 1983* (Washington, February 1982). The objectives state that the government is seeking only to support R&D as part of the purchase or production of public goods or when the private sector is unlikely to invest adequately in the national interest because benefits are not immediately "appropriate" to firms undertaking the R&D. Further, an examination of the programs described indicates that for the most part the federal government is successful in limiting government support in this way.

11   It may be argued that such incentives for R&D are not subsidies under the GATT and are therefore not trade distorting. In terms of the definition offered in Chapter 1, such incentives are TDPs even if not potentially viewed as such under the GATT and acceptable under international law.

12   OMB, *Special Analysis of the Budget,* various issues; and National Science Foundation, *Research and Development in Industry, Technical Notes and Detailed Statistical Tables,* various issues.

13   "More Tax Credits for Research Are Voted by Senate, Coming Closer to House Bill," *Wall Street Journal,* July 28, 1981, p. 5.

14   Department of Energy, *Monthly Energy Review* (May 1980), p. 77.

15   Agriculture, resource extraction, construction, and manufacturing consumed 18.0 percent of the 6.4 billion barrels of petroleum product supplied. These sectors received a subsidy equal to $2.9 billion—(0.180) (6,390,726,000)($2.59) = $2.97 billion. Manufacturing's share was computed using data on petroleum usage in the Bureau of Economic Analysis 1972 input-output tables. This procedure implicitly assumes the individual industries composing these major sectors were equally effective in reducing energy consumption from 1972 to 1976.

16   These data were obtained from the Bureau of Economic Analysis 1972 input-output tables. The use of these 1972 data to allocate the subsidy implicitly assumes that the individual industries were equally effective in reducing petroleum consumption from 1972 to 1976.

17   Residual fuel oil, middle distillate, naphtha, naphtha jet fuels, gas oils, and other specialty products were deregulated in 1976; kerojet fuel and aviation gasoline were deregulated in 1979; and butane and natural gas were deregulated in 1980.

18   DOE, *Monthly Energy Review.*

19   American Oil Company, "Decontrolling Natural Gas, Issues and Analysis" (September 1981); an independent Department of Energy study generated similar results for the impacts of deregulation on natural gas prices. Data from the American Oil Company study were used here because they provided more complete information necessary to compute a projected subsidy for the manufacturing sector in 1985.

20   The Revenue Expenditure and Control Act of 1968 restricts the tax-exempt status of IRBs to bonds defined as "small issue" (no more than $10 million, under current law) and bonds without limit that finance quasi-public services or facilities (e.g., pollution control equipment, airports, convention centers, parking garages, and sports stadiums).

21   *Daily Bond Buyer,* Municipal Finance Statistics, Statistics on State and Local Government Finance (1980).

22   And the Congressional Budget Office estimates that 70–80 percent of small issue sales are placed privately. CBO, *Small Issue Industrial Revenue Bonds* (Washington, April 1981), p. 15.

23   Ibid., pp. 23 and 24.

24 Department of Commerce, Industry and Trade Administration, "Footwear Manufacturers Take Advantage of Commerce Department Industry Revitalization Program," *Commerce News,* April 26, 1979, p. 2.

25 The effects of the financial package were not estimated by Commerce; the subsidy rate estimate for FIRP is not included in the EDA's estimated subsidy rate for SIC 31 in Table 5-2 because the program was not operational in 1976.

26 This was obtained by applying the formula in Chapter 2, footnote 8, with $e = 2.4$, $t = 1.6$ percent and $\Delta M = 7.4$ percent.

Export Promotion 4

Like other advanced industrialized countries, the United States promotes exports through direct loans, loan guarantees and insurance, tax incentives, bilateral tied aid, and other activities. This chapter examines U.S. export promotion programs,[1] which include:

- export credits—the Export-Import Bank provides direct loans, loan guarantees and insurance, and discounts loans. EXIM is assisted in its efforts by the Private Export Funding Corporation and the Foreign Credit Insurance Association;

- Overseas Private Investment Corporation—U.S. exports are promoted indirectly through OPIC loans, loan guarantees and insurance to U.S. foreign investors;

- Domestic International Sales Corporations—by establishing DISCs, U.S. firms may defer taxes on export earnings;

- tied aid—through the Agency for International Development and the Department of Agriculture, the United States employs tied bilateral aid to promote U.S. exports;

- export marketing—U.S. exports are promoted through the marketing efforts of the Department of Commerce.

U.S. efforts to promote exports parallel those of other AICs in scope, but not in magnitude. With the exception of Canada, the results presented below indicate the aid provided by other AICs' export incentives appears to be much greater than U.S. efforts, placing U.S. firms at a competitive disadvantage. Certainly, for some industries and firms, the assistance provided by these programs is significant. But across the full range of manufacturing industries, the estimates indicate that the subsidies from these programs are modest, less than 3 percent of the value of exports in 1976 and less than 2 percent in 1979. The United States also imposes export disincentives that other countries do not, further handicapping U.S. industry. While estimates of the exports lost because of these disincentives are highly speculative, they do indicate that these disincentives could conceivably offset or more than offset U.S. efforts to promote exports.

The chapter is divided into six parts. The first five describe in detail EXIM credit programs, OPIC credit programs, DISCs, U.S. bilateral tied aid, and export marketing. The sixth section presents the results and conclusions summarized in this introduction.

EXPORT CREDITS

The provision of export credits at below-market interest rates is an important policy tool of all the AICs. The subsidy implicit in concessional interest rates is often a decisive factor in determining whether a U.S. or a foreign firm makes an export sale, especially for "big ticket" items such as construction projects and capital equipment. And in some cases, export financing has been a decisive factor in the ability of foreign firms to win important sales in the U.S. market. For example, in 1982, Canadian export financing at 9.7 percent was critical in helping Bombardier win a contract for 875 subway cars with New York's Mass Transit authority at the expense of its U.S.-based competitor, Budd.

Export Credit Competition

The United States provides credit assistance to exporters through the Export-Import Bank. This assistance is designed to meet the challenge of foreign subsidized export credits but, as shown here, the assistance is small compared to that offered by other AICs. Further, as illustrated in the projections presented later in this chapter, the amount of the assistance offered is declining as a result of recent budget cuts.

Table 4-1 compares the export credit programs of the U.S. Export-Import Bank with those of its counterparts in Canada, France, the United Kingdom, West Germany, and Japan. In 1979, the United States ranked last in the proportion of exports receiving support (loans, loan guarantees and insurance). The effective cost of long-term, officially supported loans was highest in the United States and Canada and lowest in Japan.

All five other AICs in Table 4-1 offer basic insurance for political and commercial risks. All except the United States and Canada provide exchange-rate insurance to cover exchange-rate losses. Inflation insurance, covering an exporter's costs in excess of a predetermined inflation rate, is available in France and the United Kingdom.

The major industrial countries' export financing activities are governed by the International Agreement on Guidelines for Officially Supported Export Credits, which places a floor under the interest rates that may be charged according to the terms of the loans and the importing countries' economic status. However, these rates are well below market rates, and competition in the area of export financing is likely to continue.

U.S. Export Credits

U.S. export promotion efforts formally began in 1934 with the establishment of EXIM, an independent government agency, to finance trade with the Soviet Union and Cuba; by World War II, EXIM was expanded to include the whole international trading community. EXIM operates four programs that facilitate the sale of U.S. goods abroad by improving the competitive position of U.S. goods and firms vis-à-vis foreign firms: direct loans to foreign buyers, discount loans, loan guarantees, and insurance.[2]

EXIM direct loans are available to foreign buyers to enable them to purchase U.S. goods and services. This long-term financing (over five years) is usually combined with commercial loans, so the final cost to the borrower is a blend of the EXIM rate and the prevailing commercial rate. A foreign buyer using an EXIM direct loan usually pays at least 15 percent of the price of the U.S. good or service, EXIM provides a loan for about 65 percent of the cost at a current base interest rate of 8.75 to 9.25 percent (1980), and the balance is financed by private sources at market rates typically at 1 or 2 percent above the prime rate. Direct loans are usually offered in conjunction with EXIM discount loans, loan guarantees or insurance.

TABLE 4-1. A COMPARISON OF EXPORT CREDITS PROVIDED BY THE
UNITED STATES AND OTHER MAJOR COUNTRIES, 1976 AND 1979

	United States	Canada	France	United Kingdom	West Germany	Japan
Share of total exports receiving support (percent)						
1976	7	4	36	36	10	49
1979	5	6	30	39[a]	10	38[a]
Loans						
Authorizations ($ U.S. billions)						
1976	3.5	0.8	7.6	1.2	1.1	3.3
1979	4.5	—[b]	7.8[c]	1.4[c]	n.a.	3.8[c]
Typical base rates[d] (percent)						
1976	8.3–9.5	8.5–9.5	7.5[e]	8.0[f]	7.5	7.5[e]
1979	8.1–8.4	8.5	7.5[e]	7.5[f]	7.5	7.5[e]
Effective cost to borrower[g] (percent)						
1976	9.0–10.2	9.3–11.3	8.55	8.8–9.4	8.4	8.0
1979	8.3–9.3	8.8	8.55	8.3[f]	8.4	8.0
Insurance and guarantees						
Authorizations ($ U.S. billions)						
1976	5.1	1.4	21.9	10.5	10.4	32.0
1979	5.0	3.5	32.2	33.4	14.5	39.4

n.a. = not available.
a Excludes long-term loan authorizations (data unavailable for 1979).
b Included in Insurance & Guarantees Authorizations.
c 1978.
d For long-term (over five years) loans.
e This rate varies so that the blended export credit rate (composed of public and private funds) is the interest rate minimum specified in the International Arrangement on Guidelines for Officially Supported Export Credits.
f Applies to dollar-denominated export credits.
g The final blended cost to the borrower of an officially supported long-term loan after adjustments are made to add in the cost of private-sector participation (e.g., higher interest rates and bank fees).
Source: EXIM, *Report to the Congress on Export Credit Competition and the Export-Import Bank of the United States*, various issues.

EXIM discount loans are agreements to purchase medium-term loans (six months to five years) provided by private lenders at fixed interest rates. The discount loan program enables commercial banks to borrow against the outstanding amount of fixed interest rate export notes.

EXIM direct and discount loans generally finance major capital purchases by foreign customers and account for a large share of total EXIM authorizations—40 percent ($3.5 billion) in FY 1976 and 47 percent ($4.5 billion) in FY 1979 (see Table 4–2).

EXIM also guarantees the repayment of medium-term export loans provided by U.S. banks—100 percent on political risks and 90 percent on commercial risks. In FY 1976, guarantees totaled $1.7 billion, declining 45 percent to $0.9 billion in FY 1979, or 10 percent of total EXIM authorizations.

The Private Export Funding Corporation, set up in 1971 to increase private participation in exporting and to stretch EXIM's resources, is privately owned by commercial banks, industrial firms and an investment banking firm. PEFCO extends medium- and long-term loans with EXIM's unconditional guarantee at fixed or floating interest rates. Although privately owned, it is heavily reliant on EXIM to guarantee repayment on all its obligations.

Finally, working closely with a private organization, the Foreign Credit Insurance Association, EXIM insures short- and medium-term credits provided by private lenders

TABLE 4-2. EXIM AUTHORIZATIONS, FY 1975-79
($ Millions)

	1975	1976	Transition Quarter	1977	1978	1979	1980
Loans (direct and discount)	3,812.6	3,488.8	488.2	1,220.6	3,424.6	4,474.9	4,577.8
Loan guarantees	1,573.5	1,661.2	272.3	1,020.7	589.4	907.9	2,509.7
Insurance	2,928.8	3,469.9	730.5	3,358.3	3,362.4	4,108.4	5,521.7
Total	8,314.9	8,619.9	1,451.0	5,599.6	7,376.4	9,491.2	12,609.2

Source: EXIM, *Annual Report*, 1979 and 1980, pp. 14-15.

to foreign buyers. Established in 1961, FCIA is a group of more than 50 companies that protects U.S. exporters against commercial risks and lenders against political and commercial risks.

EXIM insurance authorizations were $3.5 billion in FY 1976; these increased to $4.1 billion in FY 1979, or 43 percent of total EXIM authorizations.

Table 4-3 gives the sectoral breakdown of EXIM authorizations in FY 1976. These loans primarily financed manufactured exports—97 percent of loans, 98 percent of loan guarantees and 94 percent of insurance authorizations. Over 97 percent of EXIM loans and loan guarantees financed exports from 4 of the 20 major manufacturing sectors in Table 4-3—fabricated metal products, machinery, electric and electronic equipment, and transportation equipment. In contrast, the benefits provided by insured loans are more evenly distributed across the manufacturing sector.

The estimated rates of subsidy to the exports of major industry groups afforded by all EXIM programs in FY 1976 are presented in Table 4-4. Like the credit programs evaluated in Chapter 3, the subsidies implicit in EXIM loans were evaluated by comparing the discounted present value of the payments required to service the loans at assumed market rates of interest and at the lower rates on EXIM direct, guaranteed and insured loans. The rates of subsidy on the exports of each sector were then estimated by dividing the estimated subsidy received from loans by the exports of each sector. Following these procedures, the estimated subsidy to U.S. manufactured exports by EXIM programs was about 0.71 percent.[3] (Appendix C, Table C-1, presents the subsidies estimated by using a market rate of 2 percent higher.) The sectors receiving the highest rates of subsidy on total exports were:

Major Manufacturing Sector (SIC)	Subsidy Rate
Miscellaneous manufactures (39)[4]	3.1%
Fabricated metal products (34)	2.4
Machinery, except electrical (35)	1.2
Transportation equipment (37)	0.6
Electric and electronic equipment (36)	0.4

These sectors contain some of the most competitive and export-oriented U.S. industries.

From FY 1976 to 1979, the estimated rate of subsidy received from EXIM programs declined from 0.71 percent to 0.34 percent. The future of the EXIM program

TABLE 4-3. EXIM AUTHORIZATIONS BY MAJOR SIC SECTOR, FY 1976[1]
($ Millions)

Major Manufacturing Sector (SIC)	Loans	Loan Guarantees	Insurance	Total
Food and kindred products (20)	—	*	98.5	98.5
Tobacco manufactures (21)	—	—	—	—
Textile mill products (22)	0.4	0.5	51.1	52.0
Apparel and other textile products (23)	—	—	7.4	7.4
Lumber and wood products (24)	—	—	17.8	17.8
Furniture and fixtures (25)	0.1	—	4.0	4.1
Paper and allied products (26)	0.1	0.3	103.0	103.4
Printing and publishing (27)	—	—	0.2	0.2
Chemicals and allied products (28)	16.8	6.2	151.7	174.7
Petroleum and coal products (29)	1.6	0.7	6.7	9.0
Rubber and miscellaneous plastic products (30)	—	—	28.6	28.6
Leather and leather products (31)	—	—	4.1	4.1
Stone, clay and glass products (32)	0.2	0.2	3.4	3.8
Primary metal products (33)	5.1	5.1	56.7	66.9
Fabricated metal products (34)	672.1	582.2	13.9	1,268.2
Machinery (exc. electrical) (35)	1,760.1	678.8	836.4	3,275.3
Electric and electronic equipment (36)	171.1	67.1	171.9	410.1
Transportation equipment (37)	723.5	251.4	473.5	1,448.4
Instruments and related products (38)	13.8	9.0	20.2	43.0
Miscellaneous manufactured products (39)	3.6	4.5	1,197.1	1,205.2
Total manufacturing (20-39)	3,368.5	1,626.4	3,245.9	8,240.8
Total (all sectors)	3,488.8	1,661.2	3,469.9	8,619.9

*Less than $0.05.
1 Excludes transition quarter.
Source: Compiled from EXIM, *Authorization Report, Fiscal Year 1976.*

under the Reagan Administration is presently indeterminate. The projections in the 1983 budget indicate a reduction in authorizations for loan and loan guarantee and insurance programs from 6.0 percent of total exports in FY 1980 to 4.9 percent in FY 1982 and 3.4 percent in FY 1985 (see Table 4-5). If the subsidy effect on manufactured exports declines proportionately, the estimated rate of subsidy to manufactures can be expected to fall from 0.34 percent in fiscal year 1979 to 0.30 and 0.21 percent in fiscal year 1982 and 1985. Considering the more attractive terms offered and larger amounts of exports supported by EXIM's counterparts in other industrial countries, it is difficult to see how cutting back EXIM programs would not seriously impair the competitiveness of U.S. industry.

President Reagan and the Congress are therefore considering enhancing EXIM loans and loan guarantees in the next round of budget negotiations. Given this renewed interest in export financing, the EXIM subsidy projections in Table 4-13 assume that the Administration and Congress will restore EXIM financing in 1984 and 1985 to its 1982 share of exports.

OVERSEAS PRIVATE INVESTMENT CORPORATION

U.S. exports are also promoted, more indirectly, through the loan, loan guarantee and insurance programs of OPIC.[5] A wholly owned U.S. government corporation, OPIC was created by Congress in 1969 to facilitate private U.S. investment in less developed countries by insuring U.S. investment against losses due to war or political upheavals.

TABLE 4-4. ESTIMATED RATES OF SUBSIDY PROVIDED BY SELECTED U.S. EXPORT PROMOTION PROGRAMS BY MAJOR SIC SECTOR, 1976
(Percent)

Major Manufacturing Sector (SIC)	Export-Import Bank[1]	DISCs	Tied Aid	Total Export Subsidies
Food and kindred products (20)	0.13	0.48	2.10	2.71
Tobacco manufactures (21)	—	0.69	0.16	0.85
Textile mill products (22)	0.29	0.93	0.54	1.76
Apparel and other textile products (23)	0.08	0.30	—	0.38
Lumber and wood products (24)	0.07	0.68	—	0.75
Furniture and fixtures (25)	0.17	0.33	—	0.50
Paper and allied products (26)	0.31	0.87	0.19	1.37
Printing and publishing (27)	0.003	0.83	—	0.83
Chemicals and allied products (28)	0.14	1.30	0.43	1.87
Petroleum and coal products (29)	0.06	0.42	0.07	0.55
Rubber and miscellaneous plastic products (30)	0.16	0.59	—	0.75
Leather and leather products (31)	0.13	1.36	—	1.49
Stone, clay and glass products (32)	0.03	0.70	—	0.73
Primary metal products (33)	0.15	0.42	1.03	1.60
Fabricated metal products (34)	2.35	1.01	—	3.36
Machinery (exc. electrical) (35)	1.20	1.01	0.40	2.61
Electric and electronic equipment (36)	0.41	1.39	—	1.80
Transportation equipment (37)	0.60	0.86	0.09	1.55
Instruments and related products (38)	0.09	1.32	—	1.41
Miscellaneous manufactured products (39)	3.09	1.17	1.20	5.46
Total manufacturing (20-39)	0.71	0.96	0.36	2.03

[1] Fiscal Year 1976 (excludes transition quarter).
Source: Authors' estimates.

TABLE 4-5. REAGAN ADMINISTRATION 1983 BUDGET ESTIMATES AND PROPOSALS FOR EXIM, FY 1980-86
($ Millions and Percent)

	1980[A]	1981	1982	1983	1984	1985	1986
Direct loan authorizations	$ 4,578	$ 5,431	$ 4,400	$ 3,830	$ 3,830	$ 3,830	$ 3,830
Percent of exports[1]	2.2%	2.3%	1.7%	1.4%	1.2%	1.1%	1.0%
Loan guarantee commitments and insurance	8,031	7,416	8,000	8,000	8,000	8,000	8,000
Percent of exports[1]	3.8	3.2	3.2	2.8	2.6	2.3	2.1
Total	12,609	12,847	12,400	11,830	11,830	11,830	11,830
Percent of exports[1]	6.0	5.5	4.9	4.2	3.8	3.4	3.2

A = Actual.
[1] Exports were projected using the Reagan Administration's assumed nominal GNP rates of growth.
Sources: Executive Office of the President, OMB, *Budget of the United States Government, Fiscal Year 1983* (1982), pp. 5-31; and OMB.

TABLE 4-6. OPIC-ASSISTED ACTIVITIES, FY 1976, 1978-81
($ Millions and Percent)

	1976	1978	1979	1980	1981
Investments					
Total project costs	$1,639	$665	$894	$2,481	$4,533
U.S. investors' interest	885	317	499	930	1,851
Directly generated exports	1,358	807	967	1,231	2,362
Initial procurement	(762)	(136)	(330)	(570)	(1,571)
Follow-on procurement (5 years)	(595)	(671)	(657)	(660)	(791)
Directly generated exports' share of U.S. manufactured exports	1.58%	0.74%	0.71%	0.81%	1.40%
Estimated equivalent subsidy*	0.72%	0.34%	0.32%	0.37%	0.64%

* Share of U.S. exports divided by an assumed demand elasticity for U.S. exports equal to 2.2 percent.
Sources: Investments and directly generated exports—Overseas Private Investment Corporation, *Annual Report*, various issues; shares of exports and estimated rates of subsidy—authors' estimates.

Although private-project loan guarantees may be used to purchase goods and services anywhere in the free world, direct OPIC loans are tied to procurement of goods in the United States and LDCs. Loans normally carry maturities of 5-15 years with rates that vary according to OPIC's assessment of the risk.

During FY 1976, OPIC assisted U.S. foreign investments with $885 million through direct loans, loan guarantees and loan insurance (see Table 4-6). OPIC estimated that these investments generated exports of U.S materials and equipment equal to $1.4 billion over a five-year period, or 1.6 percent of U.S manufactured exports.[6] Assuming an export demand elasticity equal to 2.2, OPIC's activities had an impact on exports equivalent to a 0.7 percent subsidy on all manufactured exports. In FYs 1978 and 1979, this subsidy effect declined to 0.3 percent, rising again in FY 1980 to 0.4 percent and in FY 1981 to 0.6 percent.[7]

The Reagan Administration's 1983 budget limits OPIC loan and loan guarantee obligations to $110 million (see Table 4-7). Therefore, the ratio of credit assistance to the value of exports will decline. If the subsidy impact on U.S. exports declines proportionately, the estimated subsidy effect on manufactured exports will fall slightly from 0.64 percent in 1981 to 0.62 in 1982.

TABLE 4-7. REAGAN ADMINISTRATION BUDGET ESTIMATES AND PROPOSALS FOR OPIC, FY 1980-83
($ Millions)

	1980A	1981	1982	1983
Direct loan obligations	5.0	10.0	10.0	10.0
Loan guarantee commitments	175.3	100.0	100.0	100.0
Total	180.3	110.0	110.0	110.0
Percent of manufactured exports[1]	0.12%	0.06%	0.06%	0.05%

A = Actual.
1 Manufactured exports are based on projections described in Table 4-5.
Source: Executive Office of the President, OMB, *Budget of the United States Government, Fiscal Year 1983 (1982)*, Appendix, pp. I-D21-I-D23.

TAX INCENTIVES PROVIDED BY DOMESTIC INTERNATIONAL SALES CORPORATIONS

The partial deferral of taxes on the export income of DISCs is a major tax expenditure set up by the Revenue Act of 1971 especially to promote U.S. exports and is the object of complaints by many U.S. trading partners that it constitutes a trade-distorting practice. A DISC is a wholly owned paper subsidiary through which the parent corporation, the sole shareholder, channels its eligible export sales. The DISC is not subject to corporate income tax, so its export income is not taxed until it is distributed to the parent corporation as dividends. A U.S. exporter funneling its export earnings through a DISC can potentially defer taxes indefinitely on 42.5 percent of its profits on exports exceeding a base level (67 percent of average export receipts over a moving four-year base period).[8]

To qualify as a DISC, at least 95 percent of the corporation's gross receipts must come from export sales or leases and other export-related investments or activities, and 95 percent of its gross assets must be export-related. Income from exports of certain products (including oil, gas, hard minerals, products subject to export control, and services unless they are incidental to the export of goods) is not eligible for DISC deferral. In addition, deferral on military export receipts is limited to half of what ordinarily would be allowed. The income allocated to a DISC is determined through DISC-parent corporation pricing rules that allow the DISC to realize taxable income in an amount not exceeding the greater of: (1) one-half the combined taxable income of the parent and DISC from qualified export sales plus 10 percent of related export promotion expenses; (2) 4 percent of qualified export receipts plus 10 percent of related export promotion expenses; (3) taxable income based upon the arm's-length price charged the DISC by its parent corporation.[9]

TABLE 4-8. DISC ACTIVITIES, 1976 AND 1979
($ Millions and Percent)

	1976	1979
Gross receipts of DISCs	$77,951	$115,790
Manufacturing	55,718	83,838
Nonmanufacturing	22,233	31,953
Net income	4,913	7,415
Manufacturing	4,482	6,811
Nonmanufacturing	431	604
Tax deferred income	1,962	2,569
Manufacturing	1,780	2,342
Nonmanufacturing	182	228
Tax savings	941.8	1,181.7
Manufacturing	854.4	1,077.3
Nonmanufacturing	87.4	104.9
Tax savings as a percent of exports	0.82%	0.66%
Manufacturing	0.96	0.75
Nonmanufacturing	0.34	0.30

Sources: Gross receipts, net income and tax deferred income—Department of the Treasury, *DISC Annual Report, 1979*, Table 5-1; tax savings (48 percent of tax deferred income in 1976; 46 percent in 1979) and tax savings as a share of exports—authors' estimates.

Before 1976, taxes could be deferred on as much as 50 percent of total profits from export sales. However, the so-called incremental rule revision of the Tax Reform Act of 1976, designed to continue the support for U.S. exports but at a smaller cost to the U.S. government, changed the method of figuring the tax deferral to 50 percent of the profits from export sales in excess of 67 percent of a four-year sales average.

In 1976, DISC gross receipts were about $78 billion, or 69 percent of total U.S. exports. The total tax savings were $942 million, providing a 0.96 percent subsidy to manufactured exports and a 0.34 percent one to nonmanufactured exports. As a result of the incremental provision, by 1979, rates of subsidy on manufactured and nonmanufactured exports declined to 0.75 and 0.30 percent, respectively (see Table 4-8).

Table 4-4 presented for 1976 estimates of the rates of subsidy from DISCs to individual manufacturing sectors.[10] DISCs extended the largest subsidies to the following sectors:

Major Manufacturing Sector (SIC)	Subsidy Rate
Electric and electronic equipment (36)	1.4%
Leather and leather products (31)	1.4
Instruments and related products (38)	1.3
Miscellaneous manufactures (39)	1.2
Fabricated metal products (34)	1.0
Machinery, except electrical (35)	1.0
Textile mill products (22)	0.9

The Tax Equity and Fiscal Responsibility Act of 1982 will reduce DISC benefits by an additional 15 percent beginning in 1983. TEFRA increased the amount of export profits a DISC must distribute to the parent corporation from 50 to 57.5 percent, thereby reducing the export income upon which taxes can be deferred from 50 to 42.5 percent.

Nevertheless, the DISC program continues to provide important benefits to U.S. exporters, and its elimination would have significant consequences. But the DISC program has long been the object of complaint by Canada and several European countries, who argue that the DISC program constitutes an exemption from direct taxation for exports and thus conflicts with GATT rules on subsidies. The issue was brought before the GATT in 1973, along with U.S. complaints about export income-tax practices maintained by France, Belgium and the Netherlands. In 1981, the GATT Council concluded that the practices of all four countries amounted to export subsidies and *in some cases* had effects that contravened each country's obligations under Article XVI:4 of the General Agreement. In response to this finding, the Reagan Administration is currently working closely with the private sector in seeking a DISC alternative or revisions that would confer the same benefits as the present DISC while bringing it into conformity with GATT requirements.

U.S. industry maintains that the DISC program is necessary to offset foreign export promotion devices.[11] But to the extent it is an offset to foreign export subsidies, it works only partially. The data presented in the concluding section of this chapter indicate that the export promotion efforts of most other AICs are substantially larger than those of the United States.[12]

TIED AID

The United States provides financial assistance to developing countries through two channels—multilateral and bilateral aid.

Development assistance, primarily loans and grants, is extended indirectly through multilateral institutions of which the United States is a member. These institutions, which include various multilateral development banks (the World Bank, the Inter-American Development Bank, the Asian Development Bank, and the African Development Bank) and other international institutions (the United Nations, for example) focus on providing economic infrastructure. U.S. contributions accounted for about 20 percent of U.S. aid outlays in FY 1979.

Bilateral aid is channeled directly to LDCs primarily through three programs: the Development Assistance Program, the Economic Support Fund, and the Food Aid Program. Aid is provided by grants and low interest loans and comprised about 80 percent of U.S. assistance outlays to LDCs in FY 1979. The United States can much more effectively promote U.S. exports through bilateral aid, as opposed to multilateral aid, and therefore the former is the focus of attention here.

Manufactured exports are promoted through the Development Assistance Program and Economic Support Fund, while agricultural exports are promoted by the Food Aid Program. The Development Assistance Program, administered by the Agency for International Development, provides loans and grants at concessional terms for projects to meet the basic needs of LDCs in South Asia and Latin America. In FY 1976, budget authority for this program was $0.7 billion and rose to $1.5 billion in FY 1979, or 35 percent of U.S. bilateral aid (see Table 4-9).

The Economic Support Fund (ESF), also administered by AID, extends loans and grants at favorable terms to promote the immediate (as opposed to the long-term) economic and political stability of countries in which the United States has special security interests. At one time called Security Supporting Assistance because of its military aid focus, the program was renamed Economic Support Fund in 1978 to reflect more development-oriented support for countries of political importance to the United

TABLE 4-9. U.S. BUDGET AUTHORITY FOR FOREIGN ASSISTANCE, FY 1976 AND 1979
($ Millions)

	1976	1979
Multilateral assistance	1,097	2,775
Bilateral assistance	3,296	4,361
Development Assistance Program	684	1,534
Economic Support Fund	1,690	2,321
P.L. 480	1,090	806
Other[1]	184	375
Offsetting items[2]	−352	−675
Total foreign aid	4,393	7,136

1 For 1976, this includes Peace Corps, International Disaster Relief, Indochina Postwar Reconstruction Assistance; for 1979, it includes Peace Corps and Refugee Assistance.
2 This category includes interest and principal payments from aid recipients.
Sources: Congressional Budget Office, *Assisting the Developing Countries: Foreign Aid and Trade Policies of the United States* (Washington, September 1980); and *The Budget of the United States Government*, FY 1977.

States. Although ESF allocations are made on the basis of political considerations, the program is geared to economic development,[13] and military aid may *not* be provided. ESF authorizations totaled $1.7 billion in FY 1976, rising to $2.3 billion in 1979 and accounting for over 50 percent of U.S. bilateral aid. Even though development projects are intended to claim the bulk of ESF funds, only 30 percent of ESF commitments went for project aid between 1975 and 1979; 27 percent was composed of cash grants and loans. The largest portion (43 percent) of ESF commitment over this period went to the Commodity Import Program.

The Food Aid Program (P.L. 480), administered by USDA and by AID, finances U.S. food exports through concessional loans and grants to LDCs, donating food to people with particular nutritional needs (e.g., children and mothers), and by requiring LDCs to invest at least 15 percent U.S. concessional financing in U.S.-approved self-help agricultural projects in LDCs. P.L. 480 shipments as a percentage of total U.S. agricultural exports have fallen significantly from their level of 29 percent in 1962 to 4 percent in 1978. Budget authorizations for the program amounted to 18 percent of total bilateral aid authorizations in FY 1979.

By specifying the conditions under which U.S. grants and loans may be used, AID programs promote U.S. exports. Specifically, through commodity eligibility lists and special rules (e.g., restrictions on the origins of products), AID can ensure that grants and loan funds issued to LDC governments and banks (which are transferred to individual importers) are used to purchase goods from U.S. suppliers.[14] The Commodity Import Program (CIP) of the ESF is an example of how the United States ties aid. ESF funds are deposited within the United States to be drawn down by countries receiving CIP funding. The purchase of military goods and certain other product categories are excluded, as are purchases of goods for which the United States is a net importer.

Table 4-10 breaks down AID-financed expenditures on U.S. commodities by major manufacturing sectors. Of the $705 million in AID financing spent by LDCs on U.S. goods in 1976, over three-quarters went to three sectors: food and kindred products (48 percent), nonelectrical machinery (20 percent), and chemicals and allied products

TABLE 4-10. AID-FINANCED EXPENDITURES ON U.S. COMMODITIES, 1975-79
($ Millions)

Major Manufacturing Sector (SIC)	1975	1976	1977	1978	1979
Food and kindred products (20)	174.0	340.7	411.3	400.9	235.4
Tobacco manufactures (21)	—	4.7	21.3	27.1	25.1
Textile mill products (22)	16.6	11.1	27.9	36.3	13.5
Paper and allied products (26)	15.9	18.0	18.0	13.4	7.9
Chemicals and allied products (28)	157.6	70.8	63.5	97.4	103.0
Petroleum and coal products (29)	30.5	1.5	6.8	21.6	23.2
Stone, clay and glass products (32)	5.6	—	—	—	—
Primary metal products (33)	41.3	27.6	9.6	28.8	54.3
Machinery (exc. electrical) (35)	173.0	141.0	145.1	166.9	195.3
Electric and electronic equipment (36)	—	—	15.5	55.6	36.0
Transportation equipment (37)	51.9	48.4	69.9	106.6	74.3
Miscellaneous manufactured products (39)	51.5	41.6	61.0	54.7	14.3
Total manufacturing (20-39)	717.7	705.2	849.7	1,009.4	782.8

Source: Agency for International Development.

(10 percent). In 1978, AID-financed expenditures on U.S. goods rose to $1 billion but fell back to about $783 million in 1979.

For 1976, Table 4-4 presented estimates of the rates of subsidy on exports that would be required to stimulate the same overall and sectoral distribution of exports.[15] The estimated overall rate of subsidy received by manufactured exports from tied aid is about 0.36 percent. This is considerably smaller than the estimated subsidies provided by EXIM, OPIC and DISCs in 1976. The sectors receiving the highest rate of subsidy were:

Major Manufacturing Sector (SIC)	Subsidy Rate
Food and kindred products (20)	2.1%
Miscellaneous manufactures (39)	1.2
Primary metal products (33)	1.0
Textile mill products (22)	0.5
Chemicals and allied products (28)	0.4
Machinery, except electrical (35)	0.4

In 1979, the manufactured exports generated by AID programs fell to 0.5 percent of total manufactured exports, down from 0.8 percent in 1976. This implies a proportionate decrease in the export subsidy provided by AID programs to 0.25 percent.

OTHER EXPORT PROMOTION PROGRAMS

Several U.S. government agencies provide a variety of market development, market assistance and other informational activities to U.S. exporters. While these programs are not large in comparison to EXIM programs or DISC tax benefits, they are integral parts of the federal government's efforts to promote U.S. exports. By reducing the cost of information (most often by offering user charges that are substantially lower than the charges for similar services provided by private sources), the government offers U.S. exporters what is in effect a subsidy that reduces the cost of their products and services on international markets and improves their competitive position.

Marketing assistance programs have three objectives: to make firms aware of exporting opportunities and the advantages of exporting; to provide information to the firms on overseas markets (laws and business regulations, potential customers and so on); and to help the U.S. firm market the product abroad (most commonly done through trade fairs and exhibits).

Table 4-11 compares the spending by the United States and four of its major competitors on export promotion through marketing assistance. The United Kingdom invested the most in this activity in 1976—the government spent $2.08 on promotion for every $1,000 of U.K. exports. France spent the second largest amount ($1.43), followed by Japan ($0.90), the United States ($0.56), and Germany ($0.15).

The marketing programs of these five countries are compared in more detail in Table 4-12 (see pp. 90-91). Most striking about the comparison is the wide variety of programs designed to help exporters with exporting opportunities.

TABLE 4-11. A COMPARISON OF INTERNATIONAL EXPORT MARKETING EXPENDITURES, 1976*

	France	United Kingdom	United States	West Germany	Japan
Total exports (billions)	$56.6	$46.0	$114.9	$103.6	$67.7
Promotion spending (millions)	80.7	95.7	64.4	15.5	60.7
Relative promotional intensity (spending per $1,000 of exports)	1.43	2.08	0.56	0.15	0.90

* Because this information is expressed in terms of U.S. dollars, changes in the value of the dollar vis-à-vis the currencies of the countries under consideration could significantly change the relationship in the export promotion expenditures.
Source: Congressional Research Service, "Export Stimulation Programs in the Major Industrial Countries: The United States and Eight Major Competitors," October 6, 1978, in H.L. Weisberg and Charles Rauch, *A Comparative Study of Export Incentives in the United States, France, the United Kingdom, Germany and Japan*, Occasional Papers (Chamber of Commerce of the United States, 1979), p. 7.

OVERVIEW

The estimated average rates of subsidy provided U.S. manufactured exports in 1976 are presented in Table 4-13 (see p. 92). Overall, these programs extended a total estimated rate of subsidy of 2.8 percent. The individual program estimates indicate that, in 1976, DISCs accounted for the largest share of the total subsidy rate, about 35 percent. EXIM and OPIC each contributed about 26 percent, while tied aid accounted for about half that amount.

While these programs are important for selected firms and industries, their overall implications for exports are small in comparison to the incentives provided by other major industrial countries. Moreover, the positive consequences of these programs may be overshadowed by the negative effects of U.S. export disincentives.

Potential Implication of Export Disincentives

In recent years, export disincentives have become a growing source of concern for business leaders seeking to market U.S. goods and services abroad. Some of the measures that constrain U.S. exports are the result of policies and legislation specifically designed to prevent the export of certain goods and technology, while others stem from efforts designed to achieve important national objectives that have the indirect effect of limiting exports. Among the practices often cited by knowledgeable observers are the Foreign Corrupt Practices Act, economic constraints imposed for foreign policy purposes, nuclear and arms export controls, restrictions on exports to communist countries, controls on the export of hazardous substances, and the application of various aspects of U.S. antitrust laws.

For some practices, the benefits received from the pursuit of important national goals may outweigh the costs when measured in terms of lost exports, while for other practices the opposite is true. But most economists believe responsibility for making ultimate judgments in this area should be left to the political process. Nevertheless, the cost in lost exports could outweigh the positive effect of the export-promoting policies described in this chapter.

Estimating the costs of export disincentives in terms of lost exports, both expected and unintended, is enormously difficult because a large portion of the effect on exports may be intangible; i.e., companies do not even attempt to seek export business because of their concern that their actions might be illegal or involve them in a bureaucratic tangle. However, in February 1980, the Carter Administration Interagency Export Disincentives Task Force reported an estimate based on "information, often unverifiable or speculative, which when pieced together suggested that all the disincentives collectively may have caused or contributed to a loss of $5-10 billion in U.S. exports in 1978.[16]

To the extent that the task force's estimates give some indication of the effects of export disincentives, they imply that their negative effects may offset the positive consequences of programs that promote U.S. exports. In 1978, $5-$10 billion was about 4.4-8.8 percent of U.S. manufactured exports. Dividing by the average elasticity of demand for U.S. manufactured exports used in this study (2.2, see Appendixes A and C), such a loss would be equivalent to a 2-4 percent tax (negative subsidy) on exports. These figures are significant when compared to the estimated average subsidy provided manufactured exports reported here for 1976 and 1979 (projected, see below) of 2.8 and 1.6 percent, respectively.[17]

Outlook for 1985

Budget data indicate that the value of U.S. manufactured exports relative to total exports declined from 1976 to 1979 and will continue under the Reagan economic program. The data in Table 4-13 show that support of U.S. exports has declined substantially since 1976, and that by 1985 the Reagan economic program could further reduce incentives to less than two-thirds of 1976 levels.

Sectoral Data

Table 4-4 showed the 1976 sectoral distribution of the estimated total export incentives provided by EXIM credit programs, DISCs and tied aid. Table 4-13 illustrates that together these programs account for about 74 percent of total export incentives. The major manufacturing sectors in Table 4-4 receiving the highest rates of subsidy were:

Major Manufacturing Sector (SIC)	Subsidy Rate
Miscellaneous manufactures (39)	5.5%
Fabricated metal products (34)	3.4
Food and kindred products (20)	2.7
Machinery, except electrical (35)	2.6
Chemicals and allied products (28)	1.9
Electric and electronic equipment (36)	1.8
Textile mill products (22)	1.8

Comparison with Other AIC Export Promotion Programs

As already discussed for export credits, the United States is not alone in offering export incentives. The data in Table 4-14 present an approximate comparison of pro-

90　Export Promotion

TABLE 4-12. COMPARISON OF INTERNATIONAL MARKET PROMOTION STRATEGIES

	France	United Kingdom	United States	West Germany	Japan
Policy Formulation Agency	Direction des Relátions Economiques (DREE), a subdivision of the Ministry of Economic Affairs and Finance.	The British Overseas Trade Board (BOTB) gives policy direction to the Department of Trade.	The Office of the U.S. Trade Representative and Commerce Department.	Economics Ministry, Foreign Affairs Ministry with regard to consulate offices abroad and overseas trade shows.	Ministry of International Trade and Investment (MITI).
Administrative Agency is that agency responsible for carrying out policy.	Centre Francais du Commerce Extérieur (CFCE) implements export expansion programs. The Comité des Manifestations Economiques à l'Etranger (CFMEE) is in charge of overseas trade fairs and shows.	The Department of Trade is responsible for budget management and staffing of export promotion activities.	Commerce Department's International Trade Administration.	Federal Office for Foreign Trade Information (BfAI), a semi-autonomous agency of the Economics Ministry.	Japan Overseas Trade Organization (JETRO).
TECHNIQUES *Export motivation programs* are those which identify potential exporters and encourage them, through special incentives, to make sales abroad.	The "New-to-Export Drive" gives NTEs, at CFCE expense, a complete diagnosis of their prospects for overseas sales. They are also given personalized assistance in conducting research and studies, as well as in making internal adjustments to reach full export potential.	The "Foundation Course in Overseas Trade" taught at local universities educates and trains businessmen in the fundamentals of exporting.	The U.S. and Foreign Commercial Service of the Commerce Department has offices in 67 countries and 48 district offices throughout the United States which give advice to local firms on exporting opportunities. These U.S. offices also support 50 District Export Councils which serve as local contacts to help stimulate business interest in overseas markets and reinforce specific Commerce programs and services. Other programs include the President's "E" and "E Star" Awards, the Export Multiplier Program and seminars to encourage exporting by small and minority-owned firms.	The federal government has no program for increasing domestic awareness of export potential. Recently, however, some state governments have begun programs to foster exports of local manufacturing companies.	JETRO maintains 29 local offices in major cities throughout Japan to give advice to small businesses interested in developing trade contacts abroad. About half of these local offices have commercial libraries for public use.
TRADE EVENTS *Trade Shows and Trade Centers* are permanent installations in foreign countries which provide exhibition space for organized shows and special events. *Trade Fairs* are temporary shows revolving around a	The CFMEE organizes all foreign trade shows including "French Weeks." In 1975 there was one trade center in Tokyo and 32 trade fairs. France also has a floating exhibition which stops at major ports in Arab countries to promote French naval and industrial products. France also provides "fair insurance," which partially reimburses	In 1976 the BOTB gave support to 270 foreign trade fairs through its Joint Venture Program. In this program the BOTB will pay roundtrip airfare for two representatives from each firm and up to 50% of the freight charges for the return of goods not sold at a fair.	The United States has, until recently, relied on trade centers as opposed to trade fairs. There were 86 trade shows in FY 1976. The government handles all aspects of the trade shows it sponsors and expects participants to pay the full cost of their expenses. It does, however, offer new-to-export firms a substantial discount (up to 43%)	The private sector operates and pays for most of the costs of traditional trade fairs. The Ministry of Economics will pay for some expenses, such as the costs of promoting the fair and the construction of exhibit booths. In 1976 there were 89 foreign trade fairs. The government does sponsor "representative shows," which are organized by	In FY 1975, JETRO organized 12 foreign trade fairs, plus 20 exhibitions abroad. It is estimated that normally about 25% of the cost of a firm participating in an overseas trade show is paid by JETRO.

Overview   91

	France	United Kingdom	United States	Germany	Japan
(trade fairs cont.) theme which travel from city to city.	French participants in trade fairs for exhibit expenses if they fail to achieve incremental sales.		on the standard $3,500 trade fair participating fee.	product and not by company. The government will pay for all expenses, but will be reimbursed for freight charges if the product on display is sold. The government also sponsors and supports business information booths.	
Trade Missions are group excursions conducted by the government to take potential exporters abroad to explore possible markets for their products.	France's trade mission program is aimed at experienced exporters who do not have significant sales in either the United States or the United Kingdom. The government offers no subsidies, only advice to those firms participating.	The BOTB will give financial support to trade missions, provided they are collective and are sponsored by a chamber of commerce or similar non-trading association.	The United States expects those firms or associations participating in a trade mission, to pay their own expenses.	Germany has no government-sponsored trade missions.	JETRO does not organize or sponsor trade missions. It will, however, underwrite part of the cost (½ airfare and per diem) for firms or associations going abroad, provided they publish a report on their findings.
Information Services include publications, libraries, and computerized services which give businessmen current information and data on overseas market and market trends.	The CFCE's primary function is to gather and disseminate information on foreign markets. This includes statistical data, market surveys, and other information on foreign firms, trade regulations, bids, and trade leads. Its major vehicle is the biweekly "Moniteur Officiel du Commerce International."	The Export Intelligence Service (EIS) is the original computerized system which gathers information on trade opportunities from foreign consulate offices and disseminates it on a subscription basis.	The U.S. Trade Opportunity System is a computer program that disseminates trade leads received from foreign trade posts. "World Trade Data Report" gives profiles on individual foreign firms. "Global Market Surveys" describe market opportunities and conditions in specific industrial sectors and foreign countries. (Worldwide Information and Trade System on line in 1982.)	The BfA maintains correspondents in major export markets throughout the world and receives additional information from the German Chambers of Commerce Abroad, as well as from foreign commercial officers. Its chief publication is the "Daily Foreign Trade News" which gives news on foreign markets and export opportunities.	JETRO's extensive information services include: 1) JETRO credit information, which is similar to the Commerce Department's "World Trade Daily Report;" 2) the computerized "International Trade Information Retrieval System" (JETAC), providing data on foreign (especially U.S.) trade and markets; 3) a major commercial library at JETRO headquarters; and 4) daily, monthly, and annual publications, some of which are written in English.
Market Research Programs take two forms: either a government agency conducts market research or the government provides support for firms or associations to do market research.	Qualifying firms receive consultation from PROMEX, the market research division of the CFCE. PROMEX will help firms develop their export strategy and will analyze those markets which appear to offer the best opportunities for the exporter.	The Export Marketing Research Scheme (EMRS) will share part of the costs (up to 2/3) for market research done by private firms or trade associations.	The Tailored Export Marketing Plans (TEMP) program is designed to furnish an entire package of market research and guidance on selling abroad, but only reaches a very limited number of firms.	The German government offers no program for individual market research.	JETRO will pay the full cost of contracted market research abroad to support small and medium-size firms. It will conduct small scale market studies at the request of trade associations and individual companies.
Foreign Buyer Programs are government invitations to potential foreign buyers to examine the domestic market and its products.	There is no foreign buyer program.	The BOTB sponsors foreign buyer programs which place a special emphasis on prospective buyers from developing countries.	The Foreign Buyers Program encourages buyer attendance at domestic trade shows, but does not support it.	Germany has no foreign buyer program.	There is a program to support foreign buyer attendance in Japan.

Source: H.L. Weisberg and Charles Rauch, *A Comparative Study of Export Incentives in the United States, France, the United Kingdom, Germany and Japan*, Occasional Papers (International Division, Chamber of Commerce of the United States, 1979), pp. 8–12. Reproduced with permission.

TABLE 4-13. SUMMARY OF SUBSIDIES TO U.S. MANUFACTURED EXPORTS: 1976 AND 1979 (ESTIMATED), 1982 AND 1985 (PROJECTED)
(Percent)

	1976	1979	1982	1985
Export credits (EXIM)	0.71	0.34[a]	0.30[b]	0.30[b]
OPIC	0.72	0.32	0.62[c]	0.56[c]
Tax incentives (DISCs)	0.96	0.75[d]	0.75[d]	0.64[d]
Tied aid	0.36	0.25[e]	0.21[e]	0.18[e]
Other export promotion	0.01	0.01[f]	0.01[f]	0.01[f]
Total	2.76	1.67	1.89	1.69

a Estimate reported in text.
b Based on a reduction in EXIM authorizations from 5.5 percent of total exports in 1979 to 4.9 percent in 1982 and 1985, respectively.
c Based on a reduction in OPIC loans from 0.06033 percent of manufactured exports in 1981 to 0.05875 in 1982, 0.05269 in 1983, and no further decline thereafter.
d Estimated DISCs subsidy declined from 0.96 percent in 1976 to 0.69 percent in 1978 as a result of the Tax Reform Act of 1976. No further change in the benefits assumed.
e Based on a decrease in Development Assistance Program and ESF budget authority for bilateral assistance (excludes administration) from 2.7 percent of manufactured exports in 1979 to 2.3 percent and 1.9 percent in 1982 and 1985, respectively.
f No change assumed from 1976.
Source: Authors' estimates.

grams in the United States and five other AICs—Canada, France, Germany, the United Kingdom, and Japan. The U.S. column contains the estimates of 1976 export promotion programs presented in Table 4-13. Approximations were made of the incentives received from comparable export credit, tied aid and other export promotion (marketing, technical assistance and so on) programs in the other five AICs.

As the data in Table 4-1 indicate, the export credit terms offered by the other AICs (except Canada) tend to be more attractive than the terms offered by the United States (see base rates), and these AIC programs tend to be larger when measured in terms of the share of exports supported. For 1976, the subsidies provided by these

TABLE 4-14. SUMMARY OF RELATIVE EXPORT INCENTIVES TO MANUFACTURING IN THE UNITED STATES AND OTHER MAJOR AICs, 1976
(Percent)

	United States	Canada	France	West Germany	United Kingdom	Japan
Export credit	0.7	0.4	7.0	1.2	2.3	5.1
Tied aid	0.4	0.2	0.5	0.1	0.6	0.2
Other (marketing, technical assistance, etc.)	*	*	0.1	*	*	0.1
Subtotal	1.1	0.6	7.6	1.3	3.0	5.4
Foreign investment insurance (OPIC)	0.7	n.a.	n.a.	n.a.	n.a.	n.a.
Tax incentives (DISCs)	1.0	n.a.	n.a.	n.a.	n.a.	n.a.
Total	2.8					

* = less than 0.05 percent.
n.a. = not available.
Source: See information as explained in text.

AICs were estimated in the same fashion as the subsidies provided by U.S. EXIM credits.[18] The results indicate that the average subsidies afforded exports by credit programs in France, the United Kingdom and Japan substantially exceed those provided exporters in Canada, the United States and Germany. The results further show that assistance to U.S. exporters is well below the combined average for the six countries studied and the average for the European countries alone.

Like the United States, other AICs use bilateral aid to promote exports. Since the focus of this study is the export promoting dimension of aid programs, Table 4-15 presents tied, partially tied and untied bilateral aid as a percent of total country exports for 1976 and 1979. Measured in these terms, the United States gave more tied bilateral aid than Germany, Japan and Canada, but less than France and the United Kingdom. In 1976, the United States extended the most partially tied bilateral aid as a percent of exports but by 1979, the United Kingdom surpassed the United States in this category.[19] In both years, the United States provided more untied bilateral aid as a percent of exports than Canada and Japan, but less than France, Germany and the United Kingdom.

In the absence of estimates of the exports generated by the other bilateral aid programs similar to that performed for the U.S. aid program described above, an index that combines the data in Table 4-15 for tied, partially tied and untied bilateral aid is required to compare the potential effects of each country's bilateral aid program. An export promotion index was computed for each country by adding 100 percent of tied bilateral aid, 50 percent of partially tied bilateral aid and 25 percent of untied bilateral aid and then dividing the sum by total country exports. For both 1976 and 1979, the index for the United States is higher than for Canada, Germany and Japan, but lower than for France and the United Kingdom. It appears that the United States probably falls somewhere in the middle in the use of bilateral aid to generate exports.

So that the potential effects of these bilateral aid programs could be compared to other export promotion efforts, an approximation of the relative magnitude of the subsidy accruing to exports by each country's bilateral aid program was computed by multiplying the estimated subsidy to U.S. exports by the ratio of each country's export promotion index to the U.S. export promotion index. For example, in 1976, the

TABLE 4-15. BILATERAL AID AS A PERCENT OF U.S. AND OTHER MAJOR AIC MERCHANDISE EXPORTS, 1976 AND 1979
(Percent)

	1976				1979			
	Tied	Partially Tied	Untied	Export Promotion Index*	Tied	Partially Tied	Untied	Export Promotion Index*
United States	1.99	0.54	0.57	2.40	1.45	0.33	0.83	1.82
Canada	1.13	0	0.20	1.18	0.82	—	0.17	0.86
France	2.30	0.43	1.94	3.00	1.98	0.30	1.45	2.49
W. Germany	0.27	0.02	1.10	0.56	0.39	0	1.32	0.72
United Kingdom	3.25	0.52	1.00	3.76	4.74	0.76	1.01	5.37
Japan	0.81	0.24	0.37	1.02	0.93	0.63	0.60	1.40

* Export promotion intensity = tied aid plus ½ of partially tied aid plus ¼ of untied aid.
Sources: OECD, *Development Cooperation*, Table B3, 1977 and 1980; and authors' estimates.

French index was 3.00 and the U.S. index was 2.40; therefore, the relative subsidy rate entered for France in the tied aid column of Table 4–14 is:

$$(0.36)\frac{3.00}{2.40} = 0.5$$

These approximations are indeed rough, and additional research in this area would be useful. Nevertheless, they indicate the importance of bilateral aid relative to export credits as an export promotion device. For all the countries studied here, it appears that export credits are by far the more important means for promoting exports.

The rates of subsidy implicit in export marketing and similar programs were estimated for the other AICs in Table 4–14 in the same way as for the United States. None of these programs generated a rate of subsidy greater than 0.1 percent. Total estimated rates of subsidy afforded by export credits, tied aid and other promotional programs in the table indicate that in 1976, U.S. export promotion efforts were significantly smaller than those of France, the United Kingdom and Japan, and the average for the European countries. Furthermore, the rough and approximate nature of the estimates for tied aid do not significantly affect this conclusion because the estimated subsidy effects of their export credit programs appear to be larger than the combined estimated subsidy effect of U.S. export credits, tied aid and other promotional activities. And under President Reagan's economic program, the gap between U.S. export promotion efforts and those of many of its trading partners will probably grow, increasing the difficulties U.S. firms face in meeting competition in world markets.

Notes

1 All data in this chapter are for calendar years, unless specifically noted as fiscal years. Prior to FY 1976, fiscal years ran from July of the previous year through June of the current year. FY 1976 ran from July 1975 through June 1976. After a transition quarter from July 1976 through September 1976, fiscal years covered October of the previous year through September of the current year.

2 This description of EXIM programs was compiled from the following sources: Export-Import Bank of the United States, *Annual Report,* various issues; EXIM, *Report to the U.S. Congress on Export Credit Competition and the Export-Import Bank of the United States,* various issues; GAO, *Financial and Other Constraints Prevent Eximbank from Consistently Offering Competitive Financing for U.S. Exports,* Report to the Congress by the Comptroller General of the United States, ID–80–16, April 30, 1980; U.S. Congress, Senate Committee on the Budget, *Tax Expenditures: Relationship to Spending Programs and Background Material on Individual Provisions,* Committee Print (September 1978).

3 As is the case with other credit subsidies evaluated in this study, these figures reflect estimates of the value received and not actual outlays.

4 Miscellaneous manufacturing (SIC 39) consists of jewelry; silverware; toys and athletic goods; pens, pencils and office and artists' materials; costume jewelry, novelties, buttons and notions; brooms and brushes; signs and advertising displays; burial caskets; linoleum and similar floor coverings; and other miscellaneous products. This sector accounts for less than 2 percent of manufactured exports.

5 This description of OPIC activities was compiled from various issues of the Overseas Private Investment Corporation's *Annual Report* and John E. Mullen, "Export Promotion: Legal and Structural Limitations on a Broad United States Commitment," *Law and Policy in International Business* (Winter 1975), p. 88 (footnote).

6   GAO notes that OPIC estimates of the benefits to the U.S. economy from OPIC-supported investments are probably overstated because they rely almost entirely on investor data (rather than independent verification) and do not take into account complicating factors such as displaced U.S. exports, possible long-term trade effects of investment-related technology transfers and stimulation of *other* industrialized country exports by U.S. investments. GAO, *The Overseas Private Investment Corporation: Its Role in Development and Trade* (February 27, 1981), p. 24.

7   This subsidy effect was computed by dividing the percentage change in exports by the export demand elasticity.

8   Department of the Treasury, *The Operations and Effect of the Domestic International Sales Corporation Legislation, 1979 Annual Report* (April 1981), p. 6.

9   Ibid., p. 5.

10   The manufacturing tax savings for 1976 were allocated to individual manufacturing sectors by employing data on the 1978 tax savings and industry distribution of DISC benefits in Department of the Treasury, *The Operations and Effect of the Domestic International Sales Corporation Legislation, 1978 Annual Report*. These sectoral tax savings are divided by sectoral exports to obtain rates of subsidy.

11   Ibid., pp. 14–16.

12   Also, many industry and labor leaders maintain that the application of border tax adjustments in Europe for value-added taxes provides additional assistance to European exporters, further increasing the gap between the export incentives received by U.S. and EC exporters.

13   From 1965 to 1974, two-thirds of ESF disbursements went to countries in East Asia, particularly South Vietnam. After 1975, the focus shifted to the Middle East; by FY 1979, 91 percent of ESF disbursements went to Egypt, Israel, Jordan, and Syria. U.S. Congress, Congressional Budget Office, *Assisting the Developing Countries: Foreign Aid and Trade Policies of the United States* (Washington, September 1980), pp. 100–101.

14   Mullen, "Export Promotion," pp. 97-98.

15   This was computed by using the formula in footnote 8, Chapter 2.

16   "Report of Working Party V to the Chairman of the Interagency Export Disincentives Task Force" (Washington, February 1980), unpublished task force report.

17   Manufactured imports were used for comparison because there was no grain embargo in place in 1978 and the other effects of these practices on other agricultural and mineral exports is quite small. Dividing $5–$10 billion by total merchandise exports would hence yield negative subsidies of 1.6 to 3.2 percent, which would not have changed the conclusions drawn in this paragraph.

18   Like the results for other credit programs, the estimated rates of subsidy are sensitive to the assumed market rate of interest. The results in Table 4–14 are based on a 10 percent market rate, the same as used elsewhere in the study for U.S. credit programs. It may be argued that the market rates for international comparisons should reflect differences in the credit market conditions of the countries studied. Several other sets of market rates were tried, all yielding very similar results.

According to the IMF, *International Financial Statistics,* interest rates were generally lower in the United States in 1976 as measured by long-term government bond rates:

United States	7.87%
Canada	9.18
France	9.16
W. Germany	7.80
United Kingdom	14.43
Japan	8.72

In one exercise, a market rate was selected for each country by adjusting the market rates assumed for U.S. export credits (10 percent) up or down on the basis of the differential from the U.S. rate:

	Assumed Market Rate	Subsidy Rate
United States	10.00%	0.8%
Canada	11.31	1.2
France	11.29	10.3
W. Germany	9.93	1.3
United Kingdom	16.56	8.7
Japan	10.85	7.2

The estimated subsidy rates for the United States, Canada and Germany remain substantially below those for France, the United Kingdom and Japan. And the United States is lowest.

Export loans are often a blend of an officially guaranteed commercial loan and an official loan. The commercial loan, being guaranteed, is risk free so it does not provide an observation for the market rate. But in another exercise, 2 percentage points were added as a risk premium to the average officially guaranteed commercial rate to obtain an assumed market rate:

	Assumed Market Rate	Subsidy Rate
United States	10.75%	1.2%
Canada	11.75	1.4
France	10.20	7.6
W. Germany	9.50	1.0
United Kingdom	10.75	3.3
Japan	9.60	4.7

Again, the subsidy rates for the United States, Canada and Germany remain substantially below those estimated for France, the United Kingdom and Japan.

19 It may be argued that intercountry comparisons of the export consequences of bilateral aid based on comparison of the volume of tied and partially tied aid tends to overstate the comparative importance of U.S. aid. The United States appears to devote relatively more of its bilateral economic aid to basic human needs—e.g., agricultural development, education, health, and social infrastructure and welfare—than do the other countries listed in Table 4-15. These countries devote more aid to public utility development and industry and mining and construction projects. Such emphasis improves the likelihood of extensive exports from the donor countries than does aid focusing on basic human needs.

Conclusions 5

During most of the postwar era, the United States has pursued policies to encourage freer trade and investment flows. Through the GATT, the United States supported gradual multilateral tariff reductions, and the resulting progress was fundamental to the dramatic postwar growth of trade among the AICs and between the AICs and developing economies of the Third World.

In recent years, slower economic growth, increasingly difficult adjustment problems in some established industries, and a perceived need in many industrial countries to pursue national policies to assure the growth of emerging high technology industries have caused many countries to turn to policies that protect domestic industry and distort international trade. Such policies include administrative practices and outright restrictions that discourage or definitely limit imports,[1] explicit and implicit domestic production subsidies, and aggressive export incentive and marketing programs. All these actions promote domestic employment and export unemployment by discouraging imports, encouraging exports, or both. As a result of growing concern about these practices, NTBs were the focus of as much attention as tariffs at the Tokyo Round negotiations, which resulted in codes to govern and limit the use of the practices.

This study has focused on the protection afforded U.S. manufacturing by NTBs. The analysis provides evidence supporting four principal conclusions.

- First, on average across the full spectrum of manufacturing, the NTBs studied here that limit or discourage imports[2] do not appear to have grown to the same importance as tariffs. Of course, for specific sectors and industries, the protection received from NTBs has been very important—e.g., book printing (the Manufacturing Clause), apparel (the Multi-Fiber Arrangement) and shipbuilding (various domestic subsidies).

- Second, on average across the full spectrum of manufacturing, U.S. programs and incentives that encourage exports[3] appear to provide benefits that are no greater, and probably less, than the protection received by import-competing industries from tariffs and nontariff barriers to imports.

- Third, for two of the three major groups of NTBs studied—domestic production subsidies and export subsidies—U.S. efforts to assist domestic industry and support domestic employment in general do not provide benefits as large as similar programs in other major AICs. Further, average U.S. tariffs tend to be lower than those of other AICs. Finally, it does not appear likely that the differences in the protection provided by U.S. and other AIC NTBs affecting producer and consumer prices would offset the imbalance of protection implied by these results.

- Fourth, the protection provided by the NTBs studied here, like tariffs, appears to be declining as a result of the agreements negotiated at the Tokyo Round and President Reagan's economic program.

U.S. NONTARIFF BARRIERS AND THE STRUCTURE OF PROTECTION

This study examined three major groups of nontariff TDPs:

- NTBs affecting producer and consumer prices, which impose quantitative constraints or other impediments on imports;
- domestic production subsidies, which promote domestic production and thereby discourage imports and encourage exports;
- exports subsidies, which, of course, encourage exports.

Table 5-1 reports for 1976 the estimated average rates of protection and subsidies afforded the entire manufacturing sector by these NTBs over and above the

TABLE 5-1. TARIFF AND SUBSIDY EQUIVALENTS OF U.S. INDUSTRIAL TRADE-DISTORTING PRACTICES, 1976 (ESTIMATED) AND 1985 (PROJECTED) (Percent)

	1976	1985
Tariffs (c.i.f.)	4.93	3.96
NTBs affecting producer and consumer prices (quantitative restrictions and safeguards, customs valuation, discriminatory excise taxes, and federal government procurement)	1.07	0.53
Domestic production subsidies (below-market credits, technical assistance, tax incentives, benefits-in-kind)	0.94	0.54
Export subsidies (below-market export credits, DISCs, OPIC, tied aid, others)	2.76	1.69
Total tariff and nontariff barriers[1]	6.71	4.83
Natural rate of protection	4.14	4.14
Total protection[1]	10.55	8.67

1 These totals are not simple sums. Rather, they are weighted averages of the factors protecting domestic industry—tariffs (T), NTBs affecting producer and consumer prices (PCP), domestic production subsidies (DPS), and the natural rate of protection (NRP)—and factors subsidizing exports—domestic production subsidies and export subsidies (XS). Total tariff and nontariff protection was computed using the following formula:

$$(T + PCP + DPS)d + (DPS + XS)(1 - d),$$

where

$$d = \frac{\text{Output} - \text{Exports}}{\text{Output}}$$

Total protection was computed using the following formula:

$$(T + PCP + DPS + NRP)d + (DPS + XS)(1 - d).$$

This is the procedure recommended by Roma Dauphin in *The Impact of Free Trade in Canada* (Ottawa: Economic Council of Canada, 1978).
Source: Authors' estimates.

protection provided by tariffs.[4] Further, it shows an estimate of the natural protection received by domestic industry from the costs created by the distance between countries (such as transportation, insurance).

The estimated combined additional protection provided by two groups of NTBs that restrict or inhibit imports—those affecting producer and consumer prices and domestic production subsidies—was only about 2 percent; this is substantially less than the protection afforded by either tariffs (about 5 percent) or natural barriers to trade (4 percent).[5] The estimated combined rate of subsidy provided manufactured industry by domestic production and export subsidies is 3.7 percent, less than the import protection arising from tariffs and nontariff barriers (about 7 percent).[6]

The modest magnitude of these estimates is particularly significant in an era in which exchange rates are heavily influenced by changes in interest rates at home and abroad and do not necessarily follow changes in production costs of U.S. firms and their competitors. Overvaluation of the dollar caused by higher U.S. interest rates could significantly reduce the overall competitive effects of these barriers on U.S. exports and imports.

Table 5-2 presents estimates of the protection received by major manufacturing sectors in 1976 from most of the NTBs examined in this study. It was not possible to compute sectoral estimates for the effects of federal procurement practices, natural gas price regulations and OPIC's impact on exports.

The estimated combined average protection from NTBs, tariffs and natural barriers included in the table was about 10 percent. Ten of the 20 sectors listed received higher than average rates of protection:

Major Manufacturing Sector (SIC)	Rate of Protection
Apparel and other textile products (23)	37.4%
Textile mill products (22)	23.7
Printing and publishing (27)	22.1
Leather and leather products (31)	17.1
Stone, clay and glass products (32)	16.8
Tobacco manufactures (21)	16.7
Rubber and misc. plastic products (30)	14.4
Miscellaneous manufactures (39)	12.6
Instruments and related products (38)	10.9
Food and kindred products (20)	10.3

This list includes many of the more labor-intense sectors of the economy.

In Chapter 1, data were presented that indicate that industries relatively more intense in the use of less skilled labor, using less capital and producing standardized products that are more vulnerable to import competition from the NICs tend to receive higher levels of tariff protection than other industries.

Once again the industries subject to GATT tariff negotiations[7] were ranked according to value-added per employee. As discussed in Chapter 1, high value-added per employee industries are generally thought to be more intense in the use of highly skilled labor, physical and R&D capital and to produce less standardized products

TABLE 5-2. SELECTED U.S. INDUSTRIAL NTB TARIFF EQUIVALENTS BY MAJOR SIC SECTOR, 1976
(Percent)

Major Manufacturing Sector (SIC)	Natural Rate of Protection	Tariffs (c.i.f.)	NTBs Affecting Producer and Consumer Prices	Domestic Production Subsidies	Export Subsidies	Total NTBs[1]	Total Protection[2]
Food & kindred products (20)	4.50	4.49	1.52	0.06	2.71	1.61	10.31
Tobacco manufactures (21)	3.57	14.52	0.04	0.02	0.85	0.13	16.74
Textile mill products (22)	6.45	18.18	0.06	0.09	1.76	0.23	23.71
Apparel & other textile products (23)	6.00	23.07	8.84	0.05	0.38	8.76	37.38
Lumber & wood products (24)	3.04	3.47	0.04	0.33	0.75	0.42	6.51
Furniture & fixtures (25)	5.83	4.11	0.04	0.11	0.50	0.16	9.92
Paper & allied products (26)	1.77	0.46	0.04	0.22	1.37	0.33	2.44
Printing & publishing (27)	3.56	1.41	17.37	0.05	0.83	17.18	22.07
Chemicals & allied products (28)	3.57	5.03	0.54	0.35	1.87	1.01	8.81
Petroleum & coal products (29)	8.99	0.65	0.04	0.10	0.55	0.15	9.68
Rubber & miscellaneous plastic products (30)	7.74	6.51	0.66	0.08	0.75	0.74	14.39
Leather & leather products (31)	8.13	9.37	0.04	0.11	1.49	0.20	17.07
Stone, clay & glass products (32)	7.02	10.10	0.10	0.22	0.73	0.34	16.83
Primary metal products (33)	4.74	3.59	0.19	0.13	1.60	0.36	8.43
Fabricated metal products (34)	2.65	5.58	0.04	0.11	3.36	0.33	8.12
Machinery (exc. electrical) (35)	4.53	4.16	0.04	0.29	2.61	0.85	7.78
Electric & electronic equipment (36)	3.64	3.61	0.04	0.32	1.80	0.56	6.99
Transportation equipment (37)	3.09	1.77	0.04	0.50	1.55	0.74	4.97
Instruments & related products (38)	2.86	9.33	0.08	0.37	1.41	0.67	10.87
Miscellaneous manufactured products (39)	4.66	8.28	0.18	0.18	5.46	0.83	12.61
Total manufacturing (20–39)	4.14	4.93	0.78	0.21	2.03	1.08	9.50

1 Total NTBs were calculated according to the following formula: (PCP + DPS)d + (DPS + XS) (1 − d), where PCP = NTBs affecting producer and consumer prices; DPS = Domestic production subsidies; XS = Export subsidies; d = (Output − Exports) / Output.
2 Total protection was computed using the following formula: (T + NRP + PCP + DPS)d + (DPS + XS) (1 − d), where T = Tariffs (c.i.f.); NRP = Natural Rate of Protection.
Source: Authors' estimates.

TABLE 5-3. AVERAGE ESTIMATED PROTECTION PROVIDED U.S. INDUSTRY:[1] QUARTILES RANKED BY VALUE-ADDED PER EMPLOYEE, 1976
(Percent)

Quartile[2]	Tariffs[3]	Total NTBs	Natural Rate of Protection	Total Protection
I	3.44	0.72	2.94	5.37
II	4.54	0.55	3.85	7.42
III	4.66	0.63	4.15	8.13
IV	13.67	2.68	6.74	21.33

1 Manufacturing, excluding food products (SIC 20), tobacco products (21) and petroleum products (29).
2 Industries were ranked by value-added per employee and divided into four equal groups by value of imports.
3 F.o.b. to maintain consistency with Table 1-2.
Source: Authors' estimates.

that are less vulnerable to competition from the NICs. In contrast, low value-added per employee industries are believed to be intense in the use of less skilled labor, and produce more standardized products. The industries were grouped into quartiles on the basis of value-added, and the estimated average rates of protection from tariffs, NTBs and natural barriers to trade were computed.

Table 5-3 shows the estimated average rates of protection afforded by tariffs, NTBs included in the previous table and natural barriers to industries with value-added per employee from the highest (Quartile I) to the lowest (Quartile IV). These estimates indicate that U.S. NTBs afford higher levels of protection to industries more intense in the use of less skilled labor. In 1976, the estimated average rates of protection provided by NTBs for which sectoral estimates were available were 2.7 percent for industries in Quartile IV and less than 1 percent for industries in Quartiles I, II and III. Furthermore, this pattern appears to be reinforced by the structure of natural protection provided by transportation and insurance costs. Therefore, the structures of tariffs, NTBs and natural barriers to trade appear to extend more protection to industries intense in use of less skilled labor.

COMPARISON OF U.S. PROTECTION TO THAT OF OTHER AICs

The data presented in this and other studies permit international comparisons of the average protection afforded industry in the AICs by three major groups of trade-distorting practices—tariffs, domestic production subsidies and export subsidies. Data on the protection provided by other AIC NTBs affecting consumer and producer prices comparable to the estimates in Chapter 2 for the United States are not available.

Table 5-4 reports estimates of the average post-Kennedy Round tariffs imposed on industrial imports by the seven major industrial countries. In this group, only Japan had lower import tariffs than the United States.[8] Further, under the Tokyo Round agreements, the United States is committed to average tariff cuts that are in general at least as large as those planned for the other major AICs; so the United States should continue to have lower tariffs than most others in this group.

TABLE 5-4. POST-KENNEDY ROUND AVERAGE INDUSTRIAL[1] TARIFF RATES[2]: SEVEN MAJOR INDUSTRIAL COUNTRIES[3]
(Percent)

United States	6.5
Canada	7.3
France	8.3
W. Germany	8.7
Italy	7.3
Japan[4]	3.9
United Kingdom	7.3
European Community (nine countries)	8.2
All industrial countries[5]	7.8

1 Includes all manufacturing except processed food, tobacco products and petroleum products.
2 Most-favored-nation applied rates.
3 Import-weighted averages employing each country's 1976 imports. Tariff rates vary within the European Community because of differences in import weights.
4 Includes pre-Tokyo Round unilateral tariff cuts.
5 Includes Australia (17.0%), Austria (15.4%), Belgium-Luxembourg (8.2%), Denmark (9.0%), Ireland (9.4%), Netherlands (9.2%), Finland (9.6%), New Zealand (18.9%), Norway (6.9%), Sweden (6.4%), and Switzerland (3.9%).
Source: Alan V. Deardorf and Robert M. Stern, *An Economic Analysis of the Effects of the Multilateral Trade Negotiations on the United States and Other Major Industrialized Countries* (Washington: U.S. Congress, Senate Finance Committee, June 1979), Table 7, p. 38.

Evidence presented in Chapters 3 and 4 suggest that the combined effects of domestic production and export subsidies of other AICs are, in general, greater than those provided by the United States. Specifically, the results reported in Chapter 3 indicate that both current account subsidies and assistance for private capital formation are lower in the United States. Further, the results of the analysis in Chapter 4 indicate that the subsidies implicit in the export credits of France, the United Kingdom and Japan substantially exceed the modest support provided exporters by the U.S. Export-Import Bank and the comparable agencies in Canada and Germany. Further, the estimates presented in Chapter 4 suggest that subsidies implicit in the export credit programs of France, the United Kingdom and Japan alone exceed the combined subsidies provided by U.S. export credits, foreign investment loan guarantees (OPIC), tied bilateral aid, and tax incentives for exports (DISCs). Most significant, the results reported in Chapter 3 (Table 3-10) indicate that both the gross subsidy benefits (including both domestic production and export credit subsidies) and the subsidy benefits net of taxes for business are lower in the United States than in the other major AICs. Of course, these estimates are approximate, and further research, especially of the practices of the other countries, would be useful.

These results for tariffs and the combined effects of domestic production subsidies and export subsidies suggest the following question: does the protection afforded by U.S. NTBs affecting producer and consumer prices offset the finding that the United States appears to provide less protection through tariffs and subsidies? This does not appear likely for three reasons. First, the estimated protection afforded by NTBs affecting producer and consumer prices evaluated in Chapter 2 only added an estimated 1 percentage point to the protection provided by tariffs. (Of course, given the rough nature of some of the estimates, protective effects as high as 2 or as low as 0.5 percentage points are certainly possible.) Second, as discussed in Chapter 2, many of the other advanced industrial countries have at times protected many of the same industries that received temporary or permanent protection from U.S. practices limiting or discouraging imports. Third, as also noted in Chapter 2, many other AICs have joined developing countries in imposing performance requirements on foreign direct investors that encourage or compel them to reduce the host country's imports or increase exports, while the United States has generally refrained from such practices. Such performance requirements distort trade and have the same kinds of consequences as quantitative restrictions and export subsidies. Moreover, since the United States is the largest source of foreign direct investment, the growth of performance requirements has particularly important consequences for American business and labor.

OUTLOOK FOR 1985

Table 5-1 presents projections of the protection arising from U.S. trade barriers likely to be in force in 1985. This table brings together the projections in Tables 2-13, 3-8 and 4-13. These projections are based on six principal assumptions:[9]

- U.S. tariffs are reduced during the 1980s as agreed to in the Tokyo Round;

- U.S. adherence to the codes governing NTBs eliminates the protection afforded by ASP and Final List customs valuation, excise taxes on distilled spirits, and two-thirds of the protection afforded by federal procurement practices;

- the protection afforded the apparel sector by the Multi-Fiber Arrangement continues at its 1973-79 level;

- President Reagan's budget reductions are implemented for the domestic production and export subsidy programs as discussed in Chapters 3 and 4 with the exception of EXIM financing;

- prices for natural gas from new sources are decontrolled in 1985 as required by the Natural Gas Policy Act of 1978;

- the restraints on Japanese motor vehicles exported to the United States are terminated before 1985;

- U.S. efforts to assist basic industries, other than those outlined above, are limited to the application of U.S. rights under the Subsidy-Countervailing Duty and Antidumping Codes and other GATT agreements governing unfair trade practices.

Essentially, these conditions assume no major change in U.S. trade policy or trade legislation. The resulting projections indicate that by 1985, the overall protection afforded U.S. manufacturing from the tariffs and NTBs studied here will likely be about 28 percent lower than in 1976. Particularly significant, those NTBs studied here that reduce imports will add only about 21 percent to the protection provided manufacturing by tariffs. The rate of subsidy to exports arising from domestic production and export incentive programs will also be only about 2.2 percent. These results suggest that if the United States continues on its present policy course, the U.S. economy will be considerably more open in 1985 than it was in 1976.

Notes

1 In this study, these restrictions have been referred to as NTBs affecting producer and consumer prices.

2 These are the NTBs affecting producer and consumer prices and domestic production subsidies.

3 These are domestic production subsidies and export subsidies.

4 As explained in Tables 5-1 and 5-2, the total protection afforded by tariffs and NTBs was computed by employing a procedure recommended by Roma Dauphin, *The Impact of Free Trade in Canada* (Ottawa: Economic Council of Canada, 1978).

5 It can be argued that the estimate in Tables 2-13 and 5-1 of the protection provided by NTBs that affect consumer and producer prices understates its importance relative to tariffs. The rates of protection reported in Table 2-13 for quantitative restrictions in place in 1976—the orderly marketing agreements for specialty steel and the Multi-Fiber Arrangement for apparel—are estimates of the rates of protection afforded over the above tariffs. It can be argued that in the absence of tariffs, these NTBs would have limited imports to 1976 levels in any case, so that they would have provided higher estimated levels of protection. Following this logic would only raise the protection afforded manufacturing by NTBs affecting producer and consumer prices reported in the two tables by less than 1 percentage point and would not substantially change the conclusions reported here.

6 This is the combined effect of tariffs, NTBs affecting producer and consumer prices and domestic production subsidies.

7 These include all manufacturing less food, tobacco and petroleum products.

8 However, Japan is noted for the maze of technical and administrative constraints it imposes on imports in place of tariffs, for which quantitative information is not available. Also, many industry and labor leaders maintain that the application of border tax adjustments in Europe significantly increases the restrictive effects of EC tariffs.

9 These assumptions are consistent with the Reagan Administration's White Paper on international trade policy. U.S. Trade Representative, *Statement on Trade Policy* (July 1981).

APPENDIX A:
Data Sources

GENERAL DATA SOURCES

Unless otherwise specified, data were obtained from the following sources:

Trade Data
U.S. export, import and tariff data for 1970-77 were obtained from an Office of Foreign Economic Research, Department of Labor printout. Data for later years, as needed, were obtained from the Department of Commerce, *U.S. Industrial Outlook,* various issues; Department of Commerce, *U.S. Imports for Consumption and General Imports* (annual), various issues, and *IM-146* (monthly), various issues.

Output Data
Output data were obtained from the INFORUM modeling project at the University of Maryland for 1975-77. Data for later years, for selected industries, were estimated using shipments data from *U.S. Industrial Outlook.*

Natural Rate of Protection
Department of Commerce, Bureau of Economic Analysis, Table D: Comparable Imports in Foreign Port Value and Domestic Port Value, 1972; "The Input-Output Structure of the U.S. Economy," *Survey of Current Business,* Vol. 59, No. 4 (April 1979).

Value-Added per Employee
Department of Commerce, *Survey of Manufactures, 1976.*

SIC-Input-Output Concordance
Department of Commerce, Bureau of Economic Analysis, Appendix I: Industry Classification of the 1972 Input-Output Tables, *Survey of Current Business,* Vol. 59, No. 4 (April 1979).

Elasticities
Margaret Buckler and Clopper Almond, "Imports and Exports in an Input-Output Model," *Proceedings of the Business and Economics Section of the American Statistical Association* (1972), pp. 175-182; Stephen P. Magee, "Prices, Incomes and Foreign Trade," in *International Trade and Finance: Frontiers for Research,* ed. Peter B. Kenen (Cambridge: Cambridge University Press, 1975).

Other
Economic Report of the President, various issues.

Office of Management and Budget, *Special Analysis of the Budget of the United States Government,* various issues.

Department of Commerce, Industry and Trade Administration, *U.S. Industrial Outlook,* various issues.

Department of Commerce, Bureau of the Census, Table 4: Exports, Imports, and Calculated Duty, by SIC Commodity Major Groups, *U.S. Commodity Exports and Imports as Related to Output,* 1976 and 1975, pp. 135-136; 1972 and 1971, pp. 238-239.

Office of Management and Budget, *Major Themes and Additional Budget Details,* various issues.

CHAPTER 2

Safeguards
International Trade Commission, Publication Numbers 852, 893, 911, 921, 933, and 1008.

_____, press releases, December 26, 1978, and January 2, 1980.

General Agreement on Tariffs and Trade, L/3700/Add.2, May 14, 1976; L/4634/Add.2, May 3, 1978; L/4702/Add.1, December 6, 1978; L/4742/Add.1, January 30, 1979; L/4759/Add.1, March 12, 1979; L/4889/Add.1, January 22, 1980.

Office of the U.S. Trade Representative, *Trade Action Monitoring System,* various issues.

Customs Valuation
U.S. Congress, Senate Committee on Finance, Subcommittee on International Trade, *MTN Studies: Part 2, No. 6, Agreements Being Negotiated at the Multilateral Trade Negotiations in Geneva—U.S. International Trade Commission Investigation No. 332-101, Analysis of Nontariff Agreements,* by the International Trade Commission, CP 96-27 (August 1979).

Excise Taxes
U.S. Congress, Senate Committee on Finance, Subcommittee on International Trade, *MTN Studies: Part 4, No. 6, Agreements Being Negotiated at the Multilateral Trade Negotiations in Geneva—U.S. International Trade Commission Investigation No. 332-101, Analysis of Nontariff Agreements,* by the International Trade Commission, CP 96-27 (August 1979).

Government Procurement
General Accounting Office, *Government Buy-National Practices of the United States and Other Countries* (1976).

CHAPTER 3

Small Business Administration

Economic Development Administration
Economic Development Administration, *Annual Report,* various issues.

FmHA
Farmers Home Administration, Business and Industry Division.

R&D
National Science Foundation, *Research and Development in Industry, Technical Notes and Detailed Statistical Tables,* various issues.

Petroleum and Natural Gas
U.S. Department of Energy, *Monthly Energy Review,* various issues.

Shipbuilding
   Maritime Administration, *Annual Report,* various issues.

Footwear
   Department of Commerce, *Footwear Industry Revitalization Program, 1980,* Annual Progress Report.

Steel
   Economic Development Administration, *Annual Report,* various issues.

CHAPTER 4

Export-Import Bank
   Export-Import Bank of the United States, *Annual Report,* various issues.
   _____ *Authorization Report, Fiscal Year 1976.*
   _____ *Report to the Congress on Export Credit Competition and the Export-Import Bank of the United States,* various issues.

OPIC
   Overseas Private Investment Corporation, *Annual Report,* various issues.

DISCs
   Department of the Treasury, *The Operation and Effect of the Domestic International Sales Corporation,* Annual Report, various issues.

Tied Aid
   Agency for International Development.

   U.S. Congress, Congressional Budget Office, *Assisting the Developing Countries: Foreign Aid and Trade Policies in the United States* (September 1980).

   OECD, *Development Cooperation,* various issues.

Appendix A

BASIC DATA

TABLE A-1. SELECTED MANUFACTURING DATA, 1976

Major Manufacturing Sector (SIC)	Output	Imports	Exports	Elasticities	
	($ Millions)			Imports	Exports
Food and kindred products (20)	187,874	7,098.2	6,183.7	1.14	2.62
Tobacco manufactures (21)	13,917	316.4	1,135.4	1.14	2.62
Textile mill products (22)	32,508	2,023.6	1,520.1	2.06	1.36
Apparel and other textile products (23)	43,642	3,288.1	669.4	3.66	1.71
Lumber and wood products (24)	34,067	2,346.3	2,173.2	1.57	1.62
Furniture and fixtures (25)	13,548	515.1	244.9	6.00	1.00
Paper and allied products (26)	46,907	3,276.0	2,536.6	1.40	3.77
Printing and publishing (27)	42,052	343.2	617.9	1.40	3.77
Chemicals and allied products (28)	104,752	3,918.9	9,831.1	1.65	1.69
Petroleum and coal products (29)	117,589	6,569.0	1,275.8	1.65	1.65
Rubber and miscellaneous plastic products (30)	32,012	2,032.7	1,358.1	6.00	1.85
Leather and leather products (31)	6,773	1,719.6	243.5	4.00	1.85
Stone, clay and glass products (32)	29,465	1,092.1	1,045.6	2.59	1.21
Primary metal products (33)	100,967	8,754.1	3,147.0	1.61	0.85
Fabricated metal products (34)	75,887	1,838.6	4,027.7	1.71	0.92
Machinery (exc. electrical) (35)	104,051	6,670.1	20,997.5	1.78	1.67
Electric and electronic equipment (36)	71,570	8,405.6	8,094.3	2.10	3.32
Transportation equipment (37)	142,995	16,067.7	18,493.7	2.58	2.90
Instruments and related products (38)	24,464	2,251.3	3,978.2	1.98	2.30
Miscellaneous manufactures (39)	15,988	2,559.6	1,430.2	2.03	2.43
Total manufacturing (20-39)	1,241,028	81,086.2	89,003.9	2.14	2.20

SIC = Standard Industrial Classification.
Sources: See Appendix A text.

TABLE A-2. LOAN AND LOAN GUARANTEE TERMS, FY 1975-78

	1975	1976	1977	1978
EXIM loans and loan guarantee rates[1] (%)	6.0	7.8	8.1	8.5
Maturity[1] (years)	6.0	8.0	6.0	7.0
Shipbuilding loan guarantee rates[2] (%)	8.60	7.64	7.30	8.23
Maturity[2] (years)	20.0	20.0	20.0	20.0
FmHA loan guarantee rates[3] (%)	11.46	9.69	9.81	10.09
Maturity[3] (years)	10.1	5.1	5.2	4.6
SBA loan rates[4] (%)	7.08	6.88	6.82	6.82
Maturity[4] (years)	11.1	13.2	13.5	12.6
SBA loan guarantee rates[4] (%)	10.33	10.07	9.51	9.87
Maturity[4] (years)	7.6	8.0	9.3	9.7
EDA loan rates[5] (%)	7.78	8.19	7.69	8.08
Maturity[5] (years)	9.3	9.0	12.7	13.0
EDA loan guarantee rates[5] (%)	11.10	9.10	8.60	10.30
Maturity[5] (years)	6.7	7.6	9.5	9.0

Sources:
1 Office of Management and Budget, *Special Analysis of the Budget*, various issues.
2 The interest rate was obtained by computing the weighted average of the individual rates for all shipbuilding loan guarantees for each fiscal year. Similar maturity data were only available for FY 1978; a weighted average of 20 years was computed for that year. But because maturities did not vary much over the years, 20 years was assumed to be reflective of FY 1975-77 as well. Data were obtained from MARAD (Office of Public Affairs) printouts of Title XI loan guarantee authorizations by date, company, rate, amount, maturity, and underwriter.
3 Weighted averages of individual loan guarantee rates and maturities by fiscal year (from Business and Industry Division computer printouts).
4 Weighted averages of rates and maturities by fiscal year (from SBA Reports Management Section computer printouts).
5 Weighted averages of interest rates and maturities were computed from data supplied by EDA's Office of Development Finance Projects.

APPENDIX B:
What Is a Trade Distortion?

An open economy achieves a long-run Pareto optimum by equating the ratios of domestic social marginal costs and domestic prices to the world terms of trade.[1]
Mathematically this requirement may be stated:

$$\frac{SMC_i}{SMC_j} = \frac{P_{di}}{P_{dj}} = \frac{P_{wi}}{P_{wj}} \qquad i, j = 1, 2, \ldots, n \qquad (1)$$

where SMC_i, P_{di}, P_{wi} are the social marginal cost, domestic price and world price of the ith good. This requirement is often stated as equality between the domestic rate of transformation (DRT), domestic rate of substitution (DRS) and foreign rate of transformation (FRT), for any two goods.

$$DRT_{ij} = DRS_{ij} = FRT_{ij} \qquad i, j = 1, 2, \ldots, n \qquad (2)$$

The FRT is the terms of trade between various pairs of goods facing private and public consumers and producers in international markets. These price ratios reflect the lowest (highest) domestic currency-denominated prices importers (exporters) face (may obtain) in the absence of exchange-rate controls. As such they are domestic port prices—c.i.f. for imports and f.a.s. for exports.

A trade-distorting practice may be defined as a (government) policy or practice that alters the prices faced by producers and/or consumers in such a way that in the absence of other market imperfections and externalities, $DRT_{ij} \neq DRS_{ij}$ or $DRS_{ij} \neq FRT_{ij}$ for any two goods i and j.[2]

Almost every government spending and tax program affects the prices paid by consumers and producers. However, many of these compensate for market imperfections or externalities and, in the absence of other distortions, actually help the economy achieve the conditions described in equations (1) and (2). For example, a government program that corrects an inequality in (1) and (2) by internalizing environmental costs or by subsidizing sectors that generate positive externalities are not trade distorting by this definition.

Under this definition, broad-based taxes and transfer programs are TDPs to the extent that they change relative prices. This makes the definition too broad and cumbersome from an empirical perspective and probably unrealistic from a policy standpoint. To narrow the scope of the definition, there are two alternatives. It may be assumed that broad-based taxes and income transfer programs are not trade distorting—this assumption is often implicit in theoretical discussions of tariffs and other trade barriers. Alternatively, it may be assumed that a social welfare function exists and the government is charged with maximizing over it. Under these circumstances, broad-based taxes and transfer programs may be viewed as welfare-maximizing exercises.

Assuming broad-based taxes and transfers are not trade distorting, TDPs may be divided into two groups. In the absence of other distortions, the first group includes practices that place a wedge between relative social marginal costs (DRT) and domestic relative prices (DRS), on the one hand, and world relative prices (FRT), on the other, but leave the relationship between social marginal costs and domestic prices unchanged. Such practices raise the price(s) of the affected product(s) received by domestic producers *and* faced by domestic consumers above world levels. A tariff is a good example of such a practice.

Again in the absence of other distortions, the second group includes practices that place a wedge between relative social marginal cost(s) and domestic relative prices for affected products but do not disturb the relationship between domestic relative prices and the world terms of trade. Such practices raise the prices received by producers above world levels, but leave prices paid by consumers at world levels. Domestic production subsidies are an example.

Not all barriers to trade are imposed by government action. Some are the natural consequence of the distance between countries—transportation, insurance and other similar costs. These factors create natural differentials between domestic and world prices, but these differentials are reflected in the world prices that compose the FRT as defined above. As such, they do not drive a wedge between the FRT, on the one hand, and the DRS and DRT, on the other. Therefore, such natural protective barriers are not included among TDPs and NTBs. The NTBs studied here are limited to those barriers to trade—other than tariffs—imposed by government intervention.

REFERENCES

This Appendix applies the theoretical framework commonly applied to the analysis of domestic distortions in an open economy. Examples include:

Bhagwati, Jagdish, V.K. Ramaswami and T.N. Srinvasan, "Domestic Distortions, Tariffs, and the Theory of Optimum Subsidy," *Journal of Political Economy* (February 1963), pp. 44–50.

Magee, Stephen P., "Factor Market Distortions, Production and Trade: A Survey," *Oxford Economic Papers* (March 1973), pp. 1–42.

Notes

1   This, of course, assumes that the country would not benefit from an optimum tariff owing to its small size and the absence of domestic distortions—e.g., less than perfect (competitive) markets, external economies and diseconomies, price and wage rigidities, imperfect information.

2   This is as strong a statement as may be made: (1) We cannot define a TDP as a practice that keeps an economy from achieving a Pareto optimum: by the Second Best Theorem, a TDP, in the presence of other distortions, may or may not permit the economy to achieve a Pareto optimum by equating DRS = DRT = FRT. (2) Putting second-best considerations aside, we may not say that a TDP lowers welfare because Pareto optimums are not unique.

APPENDIX C: Methodology

One purpose of this study is to provide initial estimates of the tariff and subsidy equivalents of nontariff practices distorting trade in manufactures so that the importance of these practices relative to tariffs and natural barriers to trade may be evaluated. As we acknowledged in the "Introduction," many assumptions and judgments were required to compute the estimates reported here; for several types of practices, the results reported should be viewed as *order of magnitude estimates* of their tariff and subsidy equivalents. Nevertheless, given the level of concern among trade policymakers and private-sector leaders about the growing importance of nontariff TDPs and the lack of any comprehensive and systematic analysis of the full range of tariff and nontariff TDPs, we believe it is useful to put forward as complete a review as possible of the data available on U.S. trade practices and, wherever possible, estimate their effects. Those familiar with the empirical analysis of trade practices are aware that such a project is an enormous undertaking; therefore, this first attempt to quantify the full range of tariff and nontariff TDPs can provide only *preliminary* estimates. It is our hope that other researchers using the data presented here will carry the work further, developing more precise estimates.

The methodologies employed to estimate the tariff equivalents of TDPs affecting producer and consumer prices presented in Chapter 2 are reviewed in section 1 of this appendix, while the methodologies used to compute the estimated subsidy equivalents of programs promoting domestic production and exports reported in Chapters 3 and 4 are discussed in section 2. Section 3 discusses the implications of the approximate nature of the reported estimates for the study's overall conclusions.

(1) TDPs Affecting Producer and Consumer Prices

Like Baldwin and his colleagues, we maintain it is most appropriate to assume that domestic import-competing products and their closest foreign substitutes are imperfect substitutes when analyzing practices that potentially reduce imports of industrial products.[1] Such a model is depicted in Figure C-1. D and S are the domestic supply and demand curves, respectively, for the import-competing good, and M_s and M_d are the supply and demand curves for imports, respectively. Present is the familiar assumption that import supply is perfectly elastic. Also, the domestic supply curve is taken to be perfectly elastic; like Baldwin and his colleagues, we believe empirical evidence supports this assumption in manufacturing for moderate changes in the quantity supplied.[2]

In the absence of tariff and nontariff protection, q of the domestic good is produced and consumed and m is imported. Imposing an *ad valorem* tariff equal to t, imports are reduced to m', D shifts to D', and q' of the domestic good is produced and consumed. A nontariff TDP may reduce imports even further. For each nontariff TDP quantified in this study, the additional protection provided by the TDP *over and above* the protection afforded by tariffs was estimated.

Nontariff barriers that affect producer and consumer prices (PCPs) affect imports by directly limiting the quantity of imports *or* by directly increasing the cost of imports to consumers and thereby reducing the quantity demanded. The TDPs analyzed in Chapter 2 may be divided between these two groups as follows:

	Directly Reducing Quantity	Directly Increasing Costs
Quantitative restrictions (Nonrubber footwear, color TVs, specialty steel, textiles and apparel, printed and published materials, and automobiles)	X	
Safeguards		
Clothespins	X	
All others (porcelain-on-steel cookware, industrial fasteners, high carbon ferrochromium, CB radios, and ceramic tableware)		X
Customs valuation (ASP, Final List and documentation costs)		X
Excise taxes (Distilled spirits)		X
Discriminatory government procurement	X	

Practices Directly Reducing Imports

A PCP that reduces imports by directly limiting the quantity imported is depicted in Figure C-2. Suppose imports are reduced to m"; the change in imports is $\Delta m = m' - m''$. As Lowinger demonstrated, the tariff having the equivalent impact on imports may be defined:

$$t_e = \frac{\Delta M (1 + t)}{e_d}$$

Where ΔM is the proportional change in imports and e_d is the import demand elasticity. Estimates of t_e may be obtained given estimates of the proportional change in imports, e_d, and the value of t.[3]

To obtain estimates of ΔM for the products subject to some form of import restriction (i.e., nonrubber footwear, color TVs, specialty steel, automobiles, textile and apparel, and clothespins) or subject to discriminatory federal procurement practices, independent econometric studies of the reduction in imports were sought. As described in the text, such independent appraisals were available for nonrubber footwear from the International Trade Commission (ITC) and for book printing from the Congressional Research Service (CRS).

For color TVs, textiles and apparel, and clothespins, estimates of ΔM were made by examining trends in import shares in recent years, and these are described in detail in Chapter 2 (except for clothespins[4]).

FIGURE C-1. THE IMPACT OF A TARIFF

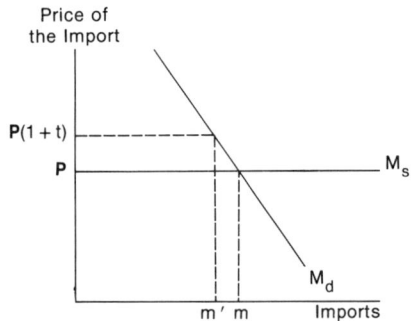
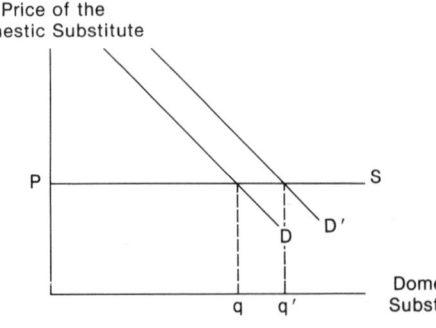

FIGURE C-2. THE IMPACT OF A PCP NONTARIFF BARRIER

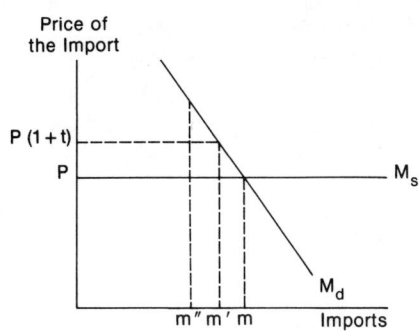
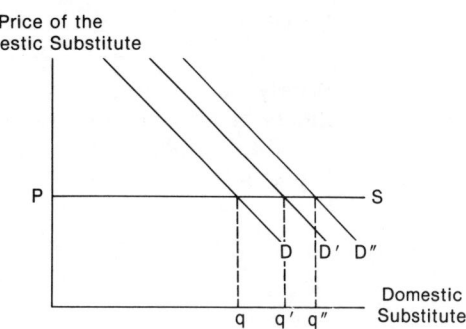

For specialty steel, as also explained in Chapter 2, the price effect of the OMA econometrically estimated for an ITC study was taken as an estimate of the tariff equivalent of that practice.

The ITC study of the nonrubber footwear industry presented an econometric model of the industry which included the following equation for imports:[5]

$$\ln(M_t) = 12.7905 + 2.3481(\ln(Y_t)) - 4.0721(\ln(P^M/P^D)_t)$$
$$(1.1174) \quad (1.8694) \quad (-4.1819)$$
$$R^2 = 0.5651 \quad D.W. = 1.4463 \quad F(2,16) = 9.7442$$

Where M, Y and P^M/P^D are imports, real disposable income and the price of imported footwear relative to domestic footwear, respectively; the values in parentheses are t ratios. Annual data were used to estimate the equation. The estimated price elasticity is highly significant and virtually equal to the estimate obtained by Buckler and Almond discussed below (−4.0). The ITC study used this equation to simulate U.S. imports for 1977–79 in the absence of the OMA and compared these values with actual imports to obtain estimates of ΔM.

The ITC study reported a similar model for color television imports but, because of several structural deficiencies, we chose not to employ its results. The estimated import demand reported was:

$$\ln(M_t) = -7.8349 + 5.0940(\ln(Y_{t-1})) - 0.6012(\ln P^M/P^D))_{t-1}$$
$$(-0.6908) \quad (3.1054) \quad (0.2981)$$
$$-0.0237(Q_{1t}) + 0.0035(Q_{2t}) + 0.0879(Q_{3t})$$
$$(-1.1348) \quad (0.016) \quad (0.8243)$$
$$R^2 = 0.8612 \quad D.W. = 1.5789 \quad F(5,7) = 9.7490$$

The model was estimated with quarterly data and Q_1, Q_2 and Q_3 are binary seasonal adjustment variables. We decided against using the estimated reduction in imports for the OMA period obtained with this equation for two reasons. First, the model focused only on complete color TVs and, as discussed in Chapter 1, analysis of the imports of the OMAs on incomplete sets and subassemblies is required to understand the full consequences of the OMA. Second, the reported price elasticity is probably biased downward by the use of only a one-period lagged observation for prices. Evidence presented by Magee indicates that prices require several quarters to have their full or even the majority of their impact on imports.[6]

In one of the most comprehensive studies of a trade-distorting practice we encountered in our research, CRS constructed a cross-section regression model to estimate the increase in imports that might be expected if the Manufacturing Clause were allowed to lapse.[7] The equation related import penetration to five explanatory variables for 73 four-digit SIC industries.

CRS Regression Results		
Variable	Coefficient	t Ratio
Constant	0.21241	3.70
Hourly wages	−0.01572	−2.07
Binary high technology variable	0.03370	1.05
Growth rate (1972–78)	−0.00559	−2.09
Export ratio	0.19297	1.53
Ratio of value-added to industry shipments	Not significantly different than zero at 90 percent	

Employing this equation, CRS researchers estimated that, in the absence of the Manufacturing Clause, imports would rise by 10–13 percent of the value of industry shipments in the long run. After examining other, noneconometric estimates, they settled on an estimate of 10–19 percent.

Many sets of estimates of U.S. import demand elasticities have been reported in the literature. Stern surveyed various studies and found that estimates of the average demand elasticity for U.S. industrial imports (manufactured imports less food and tobacco products, and mineral fuels and lubricants) varied from 0.48 to 5.00.[8] But this broad range does not imply total uncertainty about the appropriate elasticities to employ in the analysis of tariff and nontariff trade distortions. Variations in the estimates are the result of differences in the functional forms of the import demand equations estimated, the quality of the data employed in the estimation process, and the estimation technique selected. Such differences make some estimates much more reliable than others and on the basis of these considerations, Baldwin and Lewis[9] maintain that the preferred set of import demand elasticities for their analysis of the Tokyo Round tariff reductions was obtained by combining estimates obtained by Buckler and Almond and Magee.[10] Together, these studies provide elasticities for 48 different product categories, which Baldwin and Lewis assigned to the four-digit industries of the Bureau of Economic Analysis input-output model. These are the elasticities used throughout here with the exception of nonrubber footwear. (The ITC elasticity discussed above was used to estimate the tariff equivalent of the OMA in that industry.) The import-weighted average of these elasticities falls close to the middle of the range of the estimates surveyed by Stern:[11]

Import Demand Elasticity Estimates			
	Stern Survey		Buckler and Almond, Magee
	High	Low	(Baldwin/Lewis Preferred)
Food and tobacco products	3.45	0.21	1.14
Other manufacturing (excluding petroleum)	5.00	0.48	2.30

The accuracy of the estimates reported in Chapter 2 of the tariff equivalents of TDPs that directly limit imports are critically dependent on the accuracy of the estimates for the proportionate change in imports and the choice of elasticities. A 10 percent change in the estimated proportionate change in imports or assumed elasticity would result in about a 10 percent change in the results reported in Chapter 2:

	Result Reported in Text	10 Percent Increase in ΔM	10 Percent Increase in e_d
Nonrubber footwear	1.9	2.1	1.7
Color TVs	0.4–0.7	0.4–0.8	0.3–0.6
	6.7–13.4	7.3–14.7	6.0–12.0
Apparel	8.8	9.7	7.9
Printed and published material	31.2–42.4	34.3–46.6	28.4–38.5
Automobiles	2.5	2.8	2.3
Clothespins	28.2	30.1	25.5
Government procurement	0.36	0.40	0.33

Therefore, the estimates of the tariff equivalents of these TDPs reported in Chapter 2 should be viewed as order of magnitude estimates.

Practices Directly Increasing Costs

The tariff equivalents of TDPs that affect imports by directly increasing their costs were estimated by dividing estimates of the additional costs by the values of imports affected by these practices. The values of affected imports were readily available from Department of Commerce trade statistics and federal government studies of trade and production of the affected product lines. The additional costs imposed by many U.S. trade practices of this kind were easily estimated from data available from federal government studies of these practices or from federal agencies. These sources were cited in Chapter 2. Reviewing briefly:

- Safeguards

Porcelain-on-steel cookware, industrial fasteners, high carbon ferrochromium, and ceramic tableware—additional specific duties were applied to selected TSUS categories. These rates were multiplied by the quantity of imports to obtain an estimate of the total additional duty collected.

CB radios—tariffs were increased by an *ad valorem* rate; therefore, the tariff equivalent is simply the increase in the *ad valorem* tariff rate.

- Customs valuation

American Selling Price and Final List—the additional duty collected through ASP/Final List was estimated by multiplying the average *ad valorem* duty rate by the difference between the ASP/Final List valuation and f.a.s. values of affected imports.

Documentation costs imposed by U.S. Customs Invoice 5515 were estimated by the Department of Transportation by surveying the amount and cost of labor typically required to complete the form in 1971. For 1976 and 1979, this estimate was updated using a wage index for clerical workers. This estimate was in turn multiplied by the number of invoices filled out in those years to obtain the additional cost imposed by this customs form.

- Excise taxes

Excise tax on distilled spirits—the additional taxes collected as a result of the wine-gallon method of assessment were estimated by a 1979 ITC study for the Senate Subcommittee on International Trade (see Table 2-12).

Estimating the additional costs imposed on imports by U.S. safeguards, customs valuation and excise taxes was fairly straightforward; therefore, we are confident the estimates of the tariff equivalents of these practices reported in the text are reasonable.

Quality of Estimates and the Study's Conclusions about PCPs

How does the rough nature of the estimates of the tariff equivalent of PCPs that directly limit imports (quantitative restrictions and government procurement) affect the overall conclusions of the study regarding the relative importance of PCPs? Even if the estimated impacts of these practices are doubled, they still do not change our basic conclusions. Consider the results for 1976 for the average protection afforded the entire manufacturing sector:

	Result Reported in Text	Doubling Sensitive Estimates
Total PCPs	1.05	1.80
Quantitative restrictions	0.37	0.72
Safeguards	less than 0.005	less than 0.005
Customs valuation	0.21	0.21
Excise taxes	0.13	0.13
Government procurement, federal	0.36	0.72
Tariffs (c.i.f.)	4.93	4.93
Natural protective barriers	4.14	4.14

The estimated tariff equivalent of the protection provided by these PCPs over and above tariff protection is still less than half the protection provided by tariffs and natural barriers to trade. Even if the estimated effects of federal government procurement are doubled again to take into account the effects of state and local discrimination, the results do not change significantly. Moreover, it is highly unlikely that all the errors run in the same direction. It is more likely that some of the reported estimates are too high, while others are too low. Therefore, we believe our conclusions about the relative importance of the average protection provided U.S. manufacturing by the nontariff barriers affecting producer and consumer prices are fairly robust.

(2) Domestic Production and Export Subsidies

In this study, many kinds of federal domestic production and export subsidies were analyzed.

Direct payments—cash subsidies to shipbuilding.

Benefits-in-kind—technical assistance provided by the Economic Development Administration, the special Footwear Industry Revitalization Program and the Department of Commerce export marketing services; benefits to manufacturers from petroleum and natural gas price regulations.

Special tax deductions and credits—provisions assisting shipbuilding and industrial R&D; and DISCs.

Credit programs—below-market financing through direct loans and loan guarantees and insurance provided by the EDA, SBA, FmHA, the Maritime Administration, the Chrysler loan guarantee program, EXIM, and OPIC.

Tied aid—exports encouraged by tied bilateral U.S. aid.

The estimated rates of subsidy reported in Chapters 3 and 4 were obtained by dividing the estimated value of the benefits provided through these programs, on the one hand, by the value of domestic output for domestic production subsidies or the value of exports for export subsidies, on the other. The benefits created by these programs were estimated with data published or provided directly by the agencies administering the programs, the Office of Management and Budget and the Congressional Budget Office.

Direct Payments

For shipbuilding, the values of direct payments to the industry were obtained from the *Annual Reports* of the Maritime Administration.

Benefits-in-Kind

Annual federal expenditures for EDA technical assistance and Department of Commerce export marketing assistance were used as estimates of the benefits to firms from these programs. Data on the industry distribution of EDA benefits were obtained from EDA annual reports. The benefits received by the footwear and textile industries from the special Footwear Industry Revitalization Program and the Department of Commerce special textile and apparel program were included in the EDA data. We are confident that these data provide reasonably accurate estimates of the benefits to U.S. manufacturing from federal technical and marketing assistance programs.

The benefits afforded petroleum refiners and other manufacturers by crude oil price controls in 1976 and 1979 were estimated by multiplying the difference between refiners' average acquisition costs for all crude oil and for imported crude oil alone by crude runs and stills and then multiplying by the manufacturing sector's share of refined product purchases. These benefits were then allocated among manufacturing industries employing the petroleum use coefficients in the 1972 Bureau of Economic Analysis input-output tables.[12] We believe our estimates of the overall benefits to petroleum refiners and other manufacturers from crude oil price regulations are fairly accurate.

The benefits to natural gas purchasers from price regulations were computed in a fashion similar to that for crude oil price regulations. The procedure is discussed in the text and, for the reasons discussed there about the difficulties inherent in selecting an appropriate reference price for natural gas, the estimate of the overall benefits provided manufacturing is believed to be conservative.

Special Tax Deductions and Credits

The Office of Management and Budget and Congressional Budget Office annually publish estimates of the tax revenue lost through provisions of the corporate and personal tax codes that provide special benefits to individuals and firms. These sources were used to obtain historical and projected estimates of the benefits to domestic firms from tax provisions assisting shipbuilding, industrial R&D and exports through DISCs. Estimates of the tax losses created by these provisions are calculated by employing data collected from tax returns and projections of future deductions. The calculations are performed by the Treasury Department and the staff of the Joint Committee on Taxation.

Estimates of the benefits provided major manufacturing sectors by R&D tax incentives reported in Table 3-3, Chapter 3, were obtained by allocating the estimated tax benefits among U.S. industries on the basis of the industry distribution of R&D with data from the National Science Foundation.[13] Similarly, to obtain sectoral estimates of the subsidies from DISCs to U.S. exporters reported in Table 4-4, Chapter 4, the estimated tax benefits were allocated among U.S. industries on the basis of the industry distribution of DISC exports with data published by the Treasury Department in its annual report of DISC activities.

To the extent that the industry distributions of R&D and DISC tax benefits do not correspond to the industry distributions of R&D expenditures and DISC exports, respectively, some of the sectoral estimates are too high while others are too low. But, overall, individual industry errors should average out to zero.

Credit Programs

With the exception of the Chrysler loan program and the special Footwear Industry Revitalization Program, the subsidies implicit in federal programs that provide direct, guaranteed or insured loans at below-market rates were estimated by subtracting the discounted present value of the payments required to retire the loans from the discounted present value of the payments that would have been required had the loans been financed at market rates. To undertake the necessary computation, data are required for the terms of the loans (interest rate and repayment period) and for the market rate of interest that would be paid for loans in the absence of federal programs.

For each year and federal loan program studied, the average rate of interest and duration of loans were obtained for direct loans, guaranteed loans and insured loans from the agency administering the program or from the *Special Analyses of the Budget*. For FYs 1975, 1976 and 1977, the *Special Analyses of the Budget* evaluated federal subsidy programs employing market rates equal to 9.5, 10 and 10 percent, respectively; these rates were used as the market rates in this study. They are at the high end of the range of prevailing interest rates during the FY 1975-77 period:[14]

Fiscal Year	Special Analyses Market Rate	Corp. Bonds (Moody's) Aaa	Corp. Bonds (Moody's) Baa	Prime Commercial Paper (4-6 Months)	U.S. Government (10-Year Bonds)
1975	9.5	8.9	10.4	8.3	7.0
1976	10.0	8.7	10.3	5.9	7.0
1977	10.0	8.0	9.0	5.1	6.9

Since the accuracy of the estimates of the subsidies provided by these credit programs is critically dependent on the choice of a market rate, a sensitivity analysis was conducted by adding 2 percentage points to the assumed market rate; the results are reported in Table C-1 by SIC sector. For FY 1976, the average estimated rates of subsidy provided by various credit programs across the entire manufacturing sector were:

	Assumed Market Rate	Assumed Market Rate Plus 2 Percent
EDA, SBA, FmHA	0.0015%	0.0062%
Maritime Administration	0.0080	0.0155
EXIM	0.71	1.30

Raising the assumed market rate of interest by 2 percentage points raises the average subsidy from the EDA, SBA and FmHA loans by about 400 percent. But these programs account for a very small share of federal credit subsidies, and the higher value still only implies a subsidy equal to less than one-tenth of 1 percent. Raising the assumed market rate of interest by 2 percentage points approximately doubles the estimated value of the subsidies provided by the Maritime Administration and EXIM Bank.

In addition to the errors that may be imposed on the estimates of the average benefits received across all manufacturing from federal credit programs by the choice of an inappropriate market rate of interest, the sectoral estimates reported in Table 3-3, Chapter 3, for EDA, SBA and FmHA and in Table 4-4, Chapter 4, for EXIM credits may be subject to other errors arising from the way in which sectoral estimates were computed. For each program and year, the overall benefits provided were estimated and then allocated among various U.S. industries according to the industry distributions of loans, loan guarantees and insured loans. (These data were obtained from the administering agencies' annual reports or directly from the administering agency.) To the extent that, for individual major manufacturing sectors, the terms of government credits were on average more or less favorable than the terms afforded the average or typical borrower under these programs, the sectoral estimates reported in Tables 3-3 and 4-4 are underestimates or overestimates, other things being equal. These errors should average out across sectors.

Methodology

TABLE C-1. SELECTED U.S. INDUSTRIAL NTB TARIFF EQUIVALENTS EVALUATED AT R + 2%, BY MAJOR SIC SECTOR, 1976
(Percent)

Major Manufacturing Sector (SIC)	EDA, SBA, FmHA	Total Domestic Production Subsidies[1]	Export-Import Bank	Total Export Subsidies[2]	Total NTBs[3]	Total Protection[4]
Food & kindred products (20)	0.0052	0.06	0.24	2.82	1.61	10.32
Tobacco manufactures (21)	0.0017	0.02	—	0.85	0.13	16.74
Textile mill products (22)	0.0142	0.10	0.53	2.00	0.25	23.73
Apparel & other textile products (23)	0.0072	0.05	0.14	0.44	8.76	37.39
Lumber & wood products (24)	0.0175	0.34	0.13	0.81	0.43	6.52
Furniture & fixtures (25)	0.0200	0.13	0.31	0.64	0.18	9.94
Paper & allied products (26)	0.0030	0.23	0.57	1.63	0.36	2.47
Printing & publishing (27)	0.0079	0.06	0.01	0.84	17.19	22.08
Chemicals & allied products (28)	0.0034	0.36	0.26	1.99	1.04	8.83
Petroleum & coal products (29)	0.0017	0.10	0.10	0.59	0.15	9.68
Rubber & miscellaneous plastic products (30)	0.0111	0.09	0.30	0.89	0.76	14.41
Leather & leather products (31)	0.0271	0.12	0.24	1.60	0.22	17.09
Stone, clay & glass products (32)	0.0118	0.23	0.05	0.75	0.35	16.87
Primary metal products (33)	0.0037	0.14	0.26	1.71	0.38	8.45
Fabricated metal products (34)	0.0086	0.11	4.27	5.28	0.43	3.22
Machinery (exc. electrical) (35)	0.0094	0.30	2.18	3.59	1.06	7.99
Electric & electronic equipment (36)	0.0064	0.32	0.75	2.14	0.60	7.03
Transportation equipment (37)	0.0033	0.57	1.10	2.05	0.87	5.10
Instruments & related products (38)	0.0065	0.37	0.16	1.48	0.68	10.89
Miscellaneous manufactured products (39)	0.0162	0.19	5.63	8.00	1.07	12.85
Total manufacturing (20-39)	0.0062	0.23	1.30	2.62	1.14	9.56

1 Includes EDA, SBA, FmHA, R&D, petroleum, shipbuilding.
2 Includes EXIM, DISCs, tied aid.
3 Total NTBs were calculated according to the following formula: (PCP + DPS)d + (DPS + XS) (1 − d), where PCP = NTBs affecting producer and consumer prices; DPS = Domestic production subsidies; XS = Export subsidies; d = (Output − Exports)/Output.
4 Total protection was computed using the following formula: (T + NRP + PCP + DPS)d + (DPS + XS) (1 − d), where T = Tariffs (c.i.f.); NRP = Natural Rate of Protection.

As discussed in Chapter 3, the benefits afforded the Chrysler Corporation by the federal loan guarantee program were not estimated in the same way as were other federal loan programs because of the difficulties inherent in selecting an appropriate market rate for a firm that could not obtain credit under any circumstances. The impact of the Chrysler program was therefore estimated by:

- assuming that had Chrysler shut down, half its 1980 market share excluding captive imports (7.3 percent) would have been divided among domestic and foreign producers according to their 1980 market shares (67.5 and 25.2 percent, respectively); and

- estimating the tariff that would have had the equivalent impact on imports by applying the formula used for quantitative restrictions discussed above.

Assuming $e_d = 2.4$, $t = 1.7$ percent and $\Delta M = 7.3$ percent, the estimated equivalent tariff that would have restrained imports by a similar amount is 3.3 percent. So the Chrysler program may be viewed as having provided the automobile industry (SIC 3711) with the equivalent of a 3.3 percent subsidy. A 10 percent increase in ΔM would increase the estimated tariff equivalent to 3.7 percent, or by about 10 percent. Similarly, a 10 percent increase in e_d would reduce the estimated tariff equivalent to about 3.0 percent, or by about 10 percent. Doubling ΔM would increase the estimate to 7.4 percent. Assuming the imports would have captured all of Chrysler's market share, an unlikely scenario, would raise the estimate to 12.3 percent.

The subsidy to Chrysler and the automobile industry could have been estimated another way. The assistance Chrysler received may be divided into 2 groups:

- loans guaranteed by federal, state and local governments—$1,450 million;

- private-sector concessions (wage concessions, new nonguaranteed loans, dealer concessions)—$1,417.6 million.

Access to public loan guarantees permitted (and required by Congress) Chrysler to obtain additional private-sector funds. At the extreme, the federal, state and local government loan guarantees could be viewed as having a subsidy element equal to the full value of the loan guarantees—$1,450 million. This was 2.3 percent of the value of the automobile industry's shipments in 1980. This considered, the 3.7 percent estimate of the subsidy impact of the Chrysler program does not appear to be too small at all.

The subsidies to U.S. exporters from OPIC direct loan, loan guarantee and insurance programs were estimated in the same way as the subsidies implicit in U.S. tied aid, which is discussed next.

Tied Aid

As explained in Chapters 3 and 4, the United States encourages exports through OPIC and tied bilateral aid. Under the assumption that the supply of U.S. exports is infinitely elastic, the subsidy that would have the equivalent impact on exports may be estimated as follows:

$$s = \frac{\Delta X}{e_x}$$

where ΔX is the proportional change in exports and e_x is the demand elasticity for U.S. exports.

OPIC publishes estimates in its annual reports of the additional exports generated as a result of its activities. Similarly, the Agency for International Development estimates the additional U.S. exports resulting from tied aid.

As is the case with import demand elasticities, many sets of estimates of export demand elasticities have been reported in the literature. Stern's survey reported estimates for U.S. industrial export elasticities varying from 0.56 to 2.62.[15] But as with import elasticities, variations in the estimates are the result of the differences in the functional forms of export demand equations estimated, the quality of the data employed in the estimation process and the estimation technique selected. On the basis of these considerations, Baldwin and Lewis determined that the preferred set of export demand elasticities are those reported by Buckler and Almond. Again, following Baldwin's lead, the elasticities used in this study and presented in Table A-1 are the export-weighted average of these elasticities. For industrial products, these elasticities fall well within the range of estimates surveyed by Stern but, for food and tobacco products, the Buckler and Almond elasticities are somewhat higher than Stern's range.

	Export Demand Elasticities		
	Stern Survey		Buckler and Almond
	High	Low	
Food and tobacco products	2.09	0.38	2.62
Other manufacturing (excluding petroleum)	2.62	0.56	2.17

The accuracy of the estimated rates of subsidy provided U.S. exports by OPIC and bilateral tied aid are critically dependent on the accuracy of the estimates of ΔX and the choice of elasticities. A 10 percent change in ΔX or in e_x would result in about a 10 percent change in the results reported in Chapter 4 for 1976:

	Result Reported in Text	10 Percent Increase in ΔX	10 Percent Increase in e_x
OPIC	0.69	0.76	0.63
Tied aid			
Food and kindred products (20)	2.10	2.31	1.91
Tobacco manufactures (21)	0.16	0.18	0.15
Textile mill products (22)	0.54	0.59	0.49
Paper and allied products (26)	0.19	0.21	0.17
Chemicals and allied products (28)	0.43	0.47	0.39
Petroleum and coal products (29)	0.07	0.08	0.06
Primary metal products (33)	1.03	1.13	0.94
Machinery, except electrical (35)	0.40	0.44	0.37
Transportation equipment (37)	0.09	0.10	0.08
Misc. manufactures (39)	1.20	1.32	1.09

Therefore, the estimates of the subsidy equivalents of the benefits to U.S. exporters from OPIC and bilateral tied aid reported in Chapter 4 should be viewed as order of magnitude estimates.

(3) Quality of Estimates and the Study's Overall Conclusions

How does the rough nature of the estimates of the subsidy equivalents of some of the programs analyzed (natural gas price regulations, credit programs and tied aid), coupled with the approximate character of some of the estimates of the tariff equivalents of PCPs, affect the overall conclusions of this study concerning the relative importance of tariffs and nontariff TDPs? Consider the results for 1976 for the average protection afforded the entire manufacturing sector by tariffs, PCPs, domestic production subsidies, export subsidies, and natural protection when sensitive estimates[16] are doubled:

	Result Reported in Text	Doubling Sensitive Estimates
Tariffs	4.93	4.93
NTBs affecting producer and consumer prices	1.07	1.80
Domestic production subsidies	0.94	1.71
EDA, SBA, FmHA	0.0015	0.0030
R&D	0.0808	0.0808
Petroleum price regulations	0.0995	0.0995
Natural gas price regulations	0.7303	1.4606
Shipbuilding	0.0322	0.0644
Footwear	—	—
Chrysler	—	—
Export subsidies	2.76	4.55
Export credits (EXIM)	0.71	1.42
OPIC	0.72	1.44
Tax incentives (DISCs)	0.96	0.96
Tied aid	0.36	0.72
Other export promotion	0.01	0.01
Total tariff and nontariff barriers	6.71	8.28
Natural rate of protection	4.14	4.14
Total protection	10.55	12.13

Even when sensitive estimates are doubled, the average additional protection afforded manufacturing by NTBs that limit or discourage imports (PCPs and domestic production subsidies, about 3.5 percent) is less than the protection afforded by tariffs (about 5 percent). And the estimated benefits provided exporters (domestic production and export subsidies, about 6.3 percent) remain less than the protection provided import-competing industries by tariffs, PCPs and domestic production subsidies (about 8.4 percent).

Notes

1 This model is discussed in detail in Robert E. Baldwin and Wayne Lewis, "U.S. Tariff Effects on Trade and Employment in Detailed SIC Industries," *The Impact of International Trade and Investment on Employment*, A Conference on the Department of Labor Research Results, Bureau of International Labor Affairs (Washington, 1978), pp. 241–264. Some of the theoretical issues underlying the model are examined in greater depth in Robert E. Baldwin, John H. Mutti and J. David Richardson, "Welfare Effects on the United States of a Significant Multilateral Tariff Reduction" (mimeo, University of Wisconsin, April 1978).

2 Baldwin, Mutti and Richardson, "Welfare Effects on the United States," page F1, footnote 1.

3   This procedure has precedence in the literature. See Thomas C. Lowinger, "Discrimination in Government Procurement of Foreign Goods in the U.S. and Western Europe," *Southern Economic Journal* (January 1976), pp. 451–460; and Robert E. Baldwin, *Nontariff Barriers to Trade* (Washington: Brookings Institution, 1970).

4   A global quota of 2,000 gross clothespins valued at no more than $1.70 per gross was imposed on February 23, 1979. Imports surged from about 30 percent of the U.S. market in 1974 to about 42 percent in 1975 and 48 percent in 1976. Over the next 30 months, the import share was fairly stable, averaging 46.4 percent of a stable domestic market of about 6,500 gross pins per year. Assuming a continued market share of 46.4 percent in the absence of a safeguard action, the 2,000 gross clothespins quota reduced imports by about 28.2 percent.

5   ITC, *Economic Effects of Export Restraints,* ITC Report No. 1256 (Washington, 1982).

6   Stephen P. Magee "Prices, Incomes and Foreign Trade," *International Trade and Finance: Frontiers for Research,* ed. Peter B. Kenen (Cambridge: Cambridge University Press, 1975).

7   CRS, "Economic Concerns Relating to the Elimination of the Manufacturing Clause of the U.S. Copyright Law," Appendix E to the *Copyright Office's Report on the Manufacturing Clause* (Washington, 1981).

8   Stern originally reported a range of 0.48 to 10.55 but, as Baldwin later reported, the author responsible for the 10.55 estimate revised it down to about 5.00. The data presented here may be found in Baldwin and Lewis, "U.S. Tariff Effects on Trade."

9   Baldwin and Lewis, "U.S. Tariff Effects on Trade."

10   Margaret Buckler and Clopper Almond, "Imports and Exports in an Input-Output Model," *Proceedings of the Business and Economics Section of the American Statistical Association* (1972), pp. 175-184; and Magee, "Prices, Incomes and Foreign Trade."

11   For the Stern survey data see Baldwin and Lewis, "U.S. Tariff Effects on Trade," Table 2, p. 249.

12   Department of Commerce, *Survey of Current Business* (April 1979).

13   National Science Foundation, *Research and Development in Industry, Technical Notes and Detailed Statistical Tables,* various issues.

14   *Economic Report of the President,* various issues.

15   See footnote 11.

16   Estimates for PCPs directly limiting exports, natural gas price regulations, credit programs, and tied aid.

APPENDIX D:
Methodology for Estimating the Tariff Equivalents of Discriminatory Government Procurement

A methodology developed by Baldwin and Lowinger may be employed to estimate the tariff equivalents of the effects of discriminatory government procurement.[1] As it was most recently applied by Lowinger on a sector-by-sector basis, the ratios of government imports to government purchases were compared with the ratios of private-sector imports to private-sector purchases. By assuming that, in the absence of discriminatory procurement practices, the government's average propensity to import would equal the private-sector's average propensity to import, Lowinger was able to estimate hypothetical government imports in the absence of discrimination and the change in government imports (ΔM_g) imposed by discriminatory procurement practices. Assuming the tariff on government imports is equal to zero, the tariff on government imports (M_g) that would reduce M_g by the same amount may be estimated by:

$$t_g = \frac{\Delta M_g}{(M_g + \Delta M_g)e} \quad (1)$$

where e is the U.S. import elasticity of demand. It is also possible to estimate the tariff (t) on all imports (M) that would reduce M by ΔM_g:

$$t = \frac{\Delta M_g}{(M + \Delta M_g)e} \quad (2)$$

The latter concept of the tariff equivalent is of primary interest because it is the measure that is comparable to the other tariff equivalents calculated in this study.

This methodology has two drawbacks.

- To estimate the ΔM_g, t_g or t on a sector-by-sector basis, sectoral data for government procurement and government imports are required. No systematic data are collected on government purchases of foreign-made goods for use in the United States. Lowinger performed his analysis using 1962 data from a one-time only 1964 study of federal imports.

- The assumption that, in the absence of discriminatory procurement practices, government and private-sector average propensities to import would be equal is reasonable for many types of products. However, for some categories of procurement, the government purchases far more sophisticated and technologically advanced products than does the private sector. This is especially true for many categories of defense purchases from the aerospace and electronic industries.

The second problem is particularly important because defense procurement purchases account for a large share of total federal procurement (72 percent in 1979). Lowinger's estimates of t_g do not reflect this consideration and therefore are biased upward.

Lacking sectoral data on government imports, a tariff equivalent of the effects of discriminatory procurement in direct federal purchases was estimated employing the data

Methodology for Estimating Tariff Equivalents 125

for 1974 federal purchases in the 1976 GAO study cited in Chapter 2 (see Table D-1). The data permit estimates only of the average effects of discriminatory procurement across all manufacturing instead of sector-by-sector estimates, but by using this data it is possible to sort out components of federal purchases for which it is not reasonable to assume that government and private propensities to import are equal.

Table D-1 contains a breakdown of 1974 direct federal procurement by type of purchase. Coverage includes about $44.5 billion or about 90 percent, of direct federal purchases.

- $16.6 billion were effectively closed to foreign suppliers by practical constraints. These were mostly services and construction materials (an exception was a small component of construction materials, not broken out in the GAO study).

- $17.0 billion in defense purchases were limited to domestic suppliers for security reasons—e.g., maintaining an adequate defense industrial base, secrecy in R&D.

- $2.4 billion were for petroleum purchases—$1.4 billion domestic and $1.0 billion foreign.

- $2.4 billion were for Defense Department purchases abroad. These were mostly made in support of military operations abroad but $0.2 to $0.4 billion were for purchases of military equipment and R&D from U.S. allies.

- Another $3.9 billion in defense purchases were restricted to U.S. suppliers by amendments to annual appropriations legislation—these included $1.5 billion in textiles and apparel purchases.

- Another $0.4 billion in federal purchases were effectively excluded from foreign competition by minority set-asides, small business set-asides and other similar restrictions.

- The remaining $1.3 billion in general procurement were protected from foreign suppliers by Buy-American legislation.

For 1976, Table D-2 shows estimates of the imports displaced by Buy-American and buy-national legislation. The first and second columns show federal purchases that were protected from foreign competition by Buy-American or other buy-national legislation, excluding restrictions made for security reasons. In 1974, appropriations legislation restrictions excluded $3.9 billion in defense purchases from foreign competition, as did set-aside provisions for another $0.4 billion. Buy-American legislation protected another $1.3 billion. To obtain estimates for 1976, these data were scaled up by 42.4 percent to reflect the facts that the GAO covered only 88.75 percent of total procurement and that government procurement of goods grew by about 28 percent from 1974 to 1976. Column 4 shows the 1976 private average propensity to import (APM) for textiles and apparel (9.4 percent) and the private average propensity to import across all goods (6.6 percent). (These were computed with output, export and import data for major SIC industries described in Appendix A.) An estimate of the reduction in imports caused by Buy-American and other buy-national legislation was obtained by multiplying the data in column 3 by the data in column 4. The tariff that would have had the equivalent effect on total imports was estimated using formula (2), setting e equal to 2.14:

$$t = \frac{0.6308}{(81.0862 + .06308)\, 2.14}$$

$$t = 0.36\%$$

TABLE D-1. U.S. FEDERAL DIRECT PROCUREMENT OF GOODS AND SERVICES, 1974
($ Billions)

Line	Type of Purchases	
1	Purchases subject to practical constraints	16.6
2	DOD purchases subject to security restrictions	17.0
	DOD petroleum purchases	
3a	Domestic	1.4
3b	Foreign	1.0
4	DOD foreign purchases	2.4
	DOD purchases subject to appropriation bill restrictions	
5a	Textiles and apparel	1.5
5b	Other	2.4
6	Procurement subject to minority, small business and other set-aside provisions precluding participation by foreign suppliers	0.4
7	Other goods	1.3
	GAO error adjustment	0.5
	Total	44.5

Source: GAO, *Government Buy-National Practices of the United States and Other Countries* (Washington, 1976).

To put this estimate in perspective, suppose that all federal purchases of goods went to domestic producers, except for federal purchases for imported petroleum and the maintenance of U.S. military operations abroad. Further, suppose that in spite of the high technology content of defense procurement, it is only reasonable to exclude purchases subject to practical constraints (line 1 in Table D-1) from the analysis and to assume that government and private average propensities to import are equal. Then, for 1976, ΔM_g would be $2.2 billion and t would be 1.2 percent, more than triple the tariff equivalent of government procurement discrimination.

TABLE D-2. ESTIMATES OF IMPORTS EXCLUDED BY FEDERAL BUY-NATIONAL POLICIES, 1976
($ Billions and Percent)

Type of Purchase (line in Table D-1)	GAO, 1974 Procurement Data	Estimated 1976 Procurement	Private Sector APM	Effect on 1976 Imports
DOD purchases subject to appropriation restrictions				
Textiles and apparel (5a)	$1.5	$2.1	9.4%	$0.20
Other (5b)	2.4	3.4	6.6	0.22
Set-aside procurement (6)	0.4	0.6	6.6	0.04
Other goods (7)	1.3	1.9	6.6	0.12
Imports associated with federal construction (1)				0.05*
Total				0.63

* In 1974, $5.4 billion of the $134.8 billion of new construction in the United States was federally owned. Imports associated with new construction were about $618 million or only about 0.6 percent of the cost of private construction. So, in 1974, $5.4 billion in federal construction should have generated about $32 million of imports in the absence of buy-national restrictions. Scaling this figure up by 42.4 percent yields $46 million.
Source: Table D-1 and authors' estimates.

Notes

1 Thomas C. Lowinger, "Discrimination in Government Procurement of Foreign Goods in the U.S. and Western Europe, "*Southern Economic Journal* (January 1976), pp. 451–460; and Robert E. Baldwin, *Nontariff Barriers to Trade* (Washington: Brookings Institution, 1970).

National Planning Association

NPA is an independent, private, nonprofit, nonpolitical organization that carries on research and policy formulation in the public interest. NPA was founded during the Great Depression of the 1930s when conflicts among the major economic groups—business, labor, agriculture—threatened to paralyze national decisionmaking on the critical issues confronting American society. It was dedicated to the task of getting these diverse groups to work together to narrow areas of controversy and broaden areas of agreement and to provide on specific problems concrete programs for action planned in the best traditions of a functioning democracy. Such democratic planning, NPA believes, involves the development of effective governmental and private policies and programs not only by official agencies but also through the independent initiative and cooperation of the main private-sector groups concerned. And, to preserve and strengthen American political and economic democracy, the necessary government actions have to be consistent with, and stimulate the support of, a dynamic private sector.

NPA brings together influential and knowledgeable leaders from business, labor, agriculture, and the applied and academic professions to serve on policy committees. These committees identify emerging problems confronting the nation at home and abroad and seek to develop and agree upon policies and programs for coping with them. The research and writing for these committees are provided by NPA's professional staff and, as required, by outside experts.

In addition, NPA's professional staff undertakes research designed to provide data and ideas for policymakers and planners in government and the private sector. These activities include the preparation on a regular basis of economic and demographic projections for the national economy, regions, states, metropolitan areas, and counties; research on national goals and priorities, productivity and economic growth, welfare and dependency problems, employment and manpower needs, energy and environmental questions, and other economic and social problems confronting American society; and analyses and forecasts of changing international realities and their implications for U.S. policies. In developing its staff capabilities, NPA has increasingly emphasized two related qualifications. First is the development of the interdisciplinary knowledge required to understand the complex nature of many real-life problems. Second is the ability to bridge the gap between theoretical or highly technical research and the practical needs of policymakers and planners in government and the private sector.

All NPA reports have been authorized for publication in accordance with procedures laid down by the Board of Trustees. Such action does not imply agreement by NPA board or committee members with all that is contained therein unless such endorsement is specifically stated.

NPA Officers and Board of Trustees

WALTER STERLING SURREY
Chairman; Senior Partner, Surrey and Morse

MURRAY H. FINLEY
Chairman, Executive Committee; President, Amalgamated Clothing & Textile Workers' Union

DALE HOOVER
Vice Chairman; Chairman, Department of Economics and Business, North Carolina State University

JOSEPH D. KEENAN
Vice Chairman; Washington, D.C.

JOHN MILLER
Vice Chairman; Alexandria, Virginia

STEPHEN C. EYRE
Treasurer; Senior Vice President-Secretary, Citicorp

WILLIAM W. WINPISINGER
Secretary; President, International Association of Machinists & Aerospace Workers

ALEXANDER C. TOMLINSON
President; NPA

NEIL J. McMULLEN
Executive Vice President-International; NPA

SPERRY LEA
Vice President; NPA

LARRY E. RUFF
Vice President; NPA

NESTOR TERLECKYJ
Vice President; NPA

W.B. BEHNKE
Vice Chairman, Commonwealth Edison

PHILIP BRIGGS
Executive Vice President, Metropolitan Life Insurance Company

ROBERT K. BUCK
Waukee, Iowa

EDWARD J. CARLOUGH
General President, Sheet Metal Workers' International Association

SOL C. CHAIKIN
President, International Ladies' Garment Workers' Union

J.G. CLARKE
Director and Senior Vice President, Exxon Corporation

JACOB CLAYMAN
President, National Council of Senior Citizens, Inc.

G.A. COSTANZO
New York, New York

EDWARD L. CUSHMAN
Clarence Hilberry University Professor, Wayne State University

JOHN DIEBOLD
Chairman, The Diebold Group, Inc.

THOMAS W. diZEREGA
President, Northwest Energy Company

DOUGLAS A. FRASER
President, International Union, United Automobile, Aerospace & Agricultural Implement Workers of America-UAW

ROBERT M. FREDERICK
Legislative Director, National Grange

ROBERT R. FREDERICK
President, RCA Corporation

THEODORE GEIGER
Distinguished Research Professor of Intersocietal Relations, School of Foreign Service, Georgetown University

RALPH W. GOLBY
Vice President, Investor Relations, Schering-Plough Corporation

TERRY HERNDON
Executive Director, National Education Association

G. GRIFFITH JOHNSON, JR.
Executive Vice President, Motion Picture Association of America, Inc.

MARY GARDINER JONES
President, Consumer Interest Research Institute

PETER T. JONES
Senior Vice President and General Counsel, Levi Strauss & Company

LANE KIRKLAND
President, AFL-CIO

JUANITA KREPS
Durham, North Carolina

PETER F. KROGH
Dean, Edmund A. Walsh School of Foreign Service, Georgetown University

JOHN H. LYONS
General President, International Association of Bridge, Structural and Ornamental Iron Workers

LLOYD McBRIDE
International President, United Steelworkers of America, AFL-CIO, CLC

WILLIAM J. McDONOUGH
Executive Vice President and Chief Financial Officer, The First National Bank of Chicago

JOHN W. MACY, JR.
McLean, Virginia

FRANK D. MARTINO
President, Chemical Workers Union International

WILLIAM R. MILLER
President, Pharmaceutical and Nutritional Group, Bristol-Myers Company

HARRY E. MORGAN, JR.
Senior Vice President, Weyerhaeuser Company

RODNEY W. NICHOLS
Executive Vice President, The Rockefeller University

WILLIAM S. OGDEN
Vice Chairman and Chief Financial Officer, The Chase Manhattan Bank, N.A.

WILLIAM R. PEARCE
Corporate Vice President, Cargill Incorporated

GEORGE POULIN
General Vice President, International Association of Machinists & Aerospace Workers

S. FRANK RAFTERY
General President, International Brotherhood of Painters & Allied Trades

RALPH RAIKES
Ashland, Nebraska

JOHN S. REED
Vice Chairman, Citibank, N.A.

THOMAS A. REED
Group Vice President, International Control Systems, Honeywell Inc.

CARL E. REICHARDT
President, Wells Fargo Bank

WILLIAM D. ROGERS
Partner, Arnold & Porter

STANLEY H. RUTTENBERG
President, Ruttenberg, Friedman, Kilgallon, Gutchess & Associates, Inc.

HOWARD D. SAMUEL
President, Industrial Union Department, AFL-CIO

RICHARD J. SCHMEELK
Partner, Salomon Brothers

REX A. SEBASTIAN
Senior Vice President, Operations, Dresser Industries, Inc.

LAUREN K. SOTH
Journalist, West Des Moines, Iowa

ELMER B. STAATS
Washington, D.C.

MILAN STONE
URW International President, United Rubber, Cork, Linoleum and Plastic Workers of America, AFL-CIO, CLC

J.C. TURNER
General President, International Union of Operating Engineers, AFL-CIO

THOMAS N. URBAN
President and Chief Executive Officer, Pioneer Hi-Bred International

J.D. WATSON
Director, Cold Spring Harbor Laboratory

GLENN E. WATTS
President, Communications Workers of America, AFL-CIO

WILLIAM L. WEARLY
Chairman, Executive Committee, Ingersoll-Rand Company

GEORGE L-P WEAVER
Consultant, ORT Technical Assistance

LLOYD B. WESCOTT
Hunterdon Hills Holsteins, Inc.

RICHARD WARREN WHEELER
Bronxville, New York

LYNN R. WILLIAMS
International Secretary, United Steelworkers of America, AFL-CIO, CLC

ROBERT A. WILSON
Vice President, Public Affairs, Pfizer, Inc.

CHARLES G. WOOTTON
Senior Director, Public Affairs, Gulf Oil Corporation

WILLIAM H. WYNN
International President, United Food & Commercial Workers International Union, AFL-CIO, CLC

RALPH S. YOHE
Editor, Wisconsin Agriculturist

HONORARY TRUSTEES

SOLOMON BARKIN
Department of Economics, University of Massachusetts

LUTHER H. GULICK
Chairman of the Board, Institute of Public Administration

JAMES G. PATTON
Menlo Park, California